High praise for *Women in Ministry and the Writings of Paul* and for Karen Elliott, C.PP.S.! The author accomplishes well what she set out to do in this finely written and engaging book. As promised, Saint Paul and his life and culture come to life and are presented within the historical and cultural context of the first-century Church. The reader's understanding of Paul is enhanced by a careful examination of women in ministry as portrayed in Paul's writings. Elliott goes right to the heart of the issues that are frequently raised about Paul's attitude toward women and addresses them with thoughtful and studied attention. The author explores each of the many women who are referenced in Paul's writings and deftly considers their roles and functions in the establishment of the early Christian community. This is an excellent volume for undergraduate students and for use in adult education settings.

Shannon Schrein, OSF, PhD
Lourdes College, Sylvania, OH

In *Women in Ministry and the Writings of Paul*, Karen Elliott provides a sweeping sketch of women ministers from the earliest days of the church through medieval times. Highlighting the positive statements of Paul regarding women coworkers, Elliott spurs the reader to want to go deeper into the thinking of this complex apostle. Her outline of Paul's theology of baptism and of his cultural context invites reflection on the implications of Paul's writings for our own time. As she lists the names and accomplishments of influential women ministers in Christian history, Elliott encourages our continuation of their legacy.

Barbara E. Reid, OP, professor
of New Testament Studies
Vice President and Academic Dean,
Catholic Theological Union, Chicago

WOMEN
IN MINISTRY
and the
WRITINGS OF PAUL

Karen M. Elliott, C.PP.S.

ANSELM
ACADEMIC

Cover art: The seventeenth-century icon of the Myrrh-Bearing Women on the cover of this book depicts the disciples who went to the tomb of Jesus to anoint his body with myrrh oils. Five of the women are specifically named in the Gospel accounts related to this event: Mary, the *Theotokos* (in Greek, "God-bearer," the mother of Jesus), Mary Magdalene, Joanna, Salome, and Mary the wife of Cleopas (or Alphaeus). While Susanna, Mary of Bethany, and Martha of Bethany are not named in the Gospel accounts, according to tradition they are included. The Gospel accounts of these disciples ministering to Christ in the tomb are: Matthew 27:55–56, Mark 16:1, and Luke 23:55–24:1.

Image copyright © Aperges & Co, www.aperges.com; hagiographer: Holy Monastery Dormition of Theotokos Zerbitsis, Greece. Image provided by St. Isaac of Syria Skete, www.skete.com.

7028

ISBN 978-1-59982-006-4

In memory of Samuel Martin Elliott, Jr.,
my dad, my hero, and my inspiration,

and Mary Coyle Elliott,
my mom, and woman wisdom figure.

To The Sisters of the Precious Blood,
partners in Spirit-filled prayer and passionate discipleship,
women of exemplary dedication to God and to the People of God.

acknowledgments

None of us accomplishes anything alone. This statement is certainly true in my life and has been very evident during the writing of this book. This work has been a lengthy and challenging journey, the seeds of which were planted early in my childhood. Immersed in the sacred stories of people of faith, both past and present, I have become more deeply aware of and attuned to the deep abiding love that transcends time and space, a love that has inspired my research and writing.

Particularly, I am grateful to the ancestors both of my family (Ma and Pa Cope, and Grandma Coyle) and of the communion of saints (Paul, Prisca, Phoebe, Junia, Catherine of Siena, and Maria Anna Brunner). I give praise and thanks to God for my loving and supportive family, Mom and Dad (who in life and in death inspire me); my brothers, Sam, Michael, and Steven; my sister-in-law, Donna; my nieces and nephews, Terri, Sammy, Mark, Julie, Jennie, Vivien, and Hannah Mary; as well as my cousins who have graced my life with their encouragement and caring, especially Mary Agnes, Jeannette, Connie, and Carolyn.

I am grateful for the members of my religious community, The Sisters of the Precious Blood of Dayton, Ohio, who are a profound presence of the sacred and the holy in my life.

During my years of ministry I have been inspired by many faith-filled and dedicated people including the communities of St. Michael the Archangel Parish, Findlay, Ohio; Most Pure Heart of Mary Parish, Shelby, Ohio; participants in the Lay Pastoral Ministry Program in the Catholic Diocese of Toledo; and Mercy College of Northwest Ohio in Toledo. I have been graced and enriched by these communities and by their hunger to learn more of the Word of God.

As a lifelong student, I am grateful to all teachers who encouraged my love of Scripture in my formal education, and to my own students, my most compelling teachers.

I owe a debt of gratitude that can never be repaid to my dedicated friends and editors, Barbara A. Davis, SC, Carolyn Davis, Lee Krähenbühl, PhD., and Abby Weaver, along with Jerry Ruff, Paul Peterson, and Donna Crilly, the editors at Anselm Academic, who thoughtfully reviewed and revised the pages of this text.

In gratitude for all of the people who have blessed my life and ministry, I pray in Paul's words: "I give thanks to my God at every remembrance of you, praying always with joy in my every prayer for all of you, because of your partnership for the gospel from the first day until now" (Philippians 1:3–5).

PUBLISHER ACKNOWLEDGMENTS

Thank you to the following individuals who reviewed this work in progress:

Joy Milos, CSJ, PhD, Gonzaga University, Spokane, WA

Susan Myers, PhD, University of St. Thomas, Saint Paul, MN

Paul Peterson, MA, Boston University, Boston, MA

contents

preface

We live in an age in which most of us use the World Wide Web daily, spout jargon such as "global economy" and "world politics," and have international communications at a mouse-click. In spite of the global information so readily available to us, however, many of us focus on the microcosm and the frenetic pace of our daily lives. As a result, our world often becomes small and insular. We insulate our perceptions of history, restricting our thinking and actions to only what we have learned or remember. We similarly insulate our perceptions of food, politics, culture, ethnicity, economics, worship, and faith. To the extent that we insulate our perceptions, we limit our understanding.

The Apostle Paul implores the early Christian communities not to be insular. He urges them to eliminate the divisions that impede their faith. In Galatians 3:27–28, Paul pleads with the Christian communities to focus on their oneness in Christ Jesus. He insists that the Spirit given to each one in baptism eradicates political and cultural divisions. He commands them to let go of the entitlements and privileges of wealth and to have concern for the poor, the widow, and the orphan. And he urges them to abolish the gender biases that exist in every historical and cultural context. Implicit in this latter entreaty is Paul's openness to recognize the contributions and possibilities for both women and men to proclaim the gospel message and to minister to God's people.

The sacred texts, particularly the Gospels, Acts of the Apostles, and the writings of Paul, abound with stories of women engaged in such ministry. Other writings from the first century, as well as historical documents through the ages, substantiate the significant engagement of women as faith-filled followers of Jesus, the Christ, proclaiming the gospel message.

This book attempts to respond to issues of ministry being discussed within the Christian community, particularly as they apply to women. Dialogue, study, and prayer gave birth to this book, for it is through listening to one another, careful reflection on the texts of Sacred Scripture, and the prayerful creation of new and imaginative paradigms that one can best engender hope: hope that leads one to embrace the diversity of gifts and talents within Christian communities of faith; hope that recognizes the endless possibilities and variations within the people of God; hope inspired by the sacred texts of the Christian tradition that call believers, male and female, to be faith-filled followers of Jesus Christ; and hope in God, who graces with the gift of the Holy Spirit and empowers all communities of faith around the world.

I invite you, whatever your religious background or belief, to encounter here the witness of women of faith throughout the ages, and to encounter Paul, the passionate disciple of Jesus Christ who urged the early Christian communities to focus on oneness in Christ Jesus rather than on that which separates and divides. Paul wrote, "For all of you who were baptized into Christ have clothed yourselves with Christ. There is neither Jew nor Greek, there is neither slave nor free person, there is not male and female; for you are all one in Christ Jesus" (Galatians 3:27–28).[1]

---

1. All quotes from Scripture are from the *New American Bible*, 1990, unless otherwise indicated.

introduction

Some of my earliest memories of family gatherings are of the children playing and the adults sitting around the kitchen table talking. As children inevitably do, I would sit on the fringes of the adult conversation, listening. In my working-class family, the adult conversation at some point would focus on religion, and when that happened, the intensity and passion of the conversation would grow dramatically. I listened and marveled at how conversant especially my Protestant relatives were with the Bible. This sparked a desire in me to learn, to understand, and to become knowledgeable about the Bible. I wanted to be able to join in the conversation with the grown-ups and to use the sacred Scripture to assert and to confirm my position about the things that mattered to me.

With this desire to know more of Scripture, I attended my parish Catholic school as well as Vacation Bible School in the summers at both the Methodist Church and the Church of Christ. It was during Bible school that I first learned about a fiery, passionate, zealous disciple of Jesus named Paul, a man who travelled extensively, enduring misunderstanding, rejection, physical suffering, imprisonment, and numerous other hardships in his passionate fervor to preach the good news of Jesus Christ.

My first perceptions of Paul were favorable. I found him a compelling and amazing figure, someone whom I wished to emulate in my own Christian discipleship. Yet I also heard whisperings of dissent about Paul and even explicit dislike from adults who said that Paul was "too bold" and "too outspoken." However, I had heard similar criticisms about my adult role models. My dad was a fiery and passionate semi-truck driver, my mother a fiercely courageous and direct "systems and operations director" of our home. In my family experience, to be bold and outspoken were qualities to embrace and emulate, not character flaws to avoid.

I emulated others as well. Among my favorites were those I read about in the many biographies and autobiographies I always looked for in the bookmobile. I read story upon story of people who struggled against all odds and who overcame adversity. I clearly remember identifying with these amazing women and men whose lives seemed thwarted by overwhelming obstacles. Yet an undefined, mysterious inner energy graced them with the ability to demonstrate faith, courage, determination, and hope in their lives. These were great women and men, a veritable "litany of saints": Harriett Tubman, Wilma Rudolph, Jackie Robinson, Rosa Parks, Helen Keller, Indira Gandhi, Jessie Owens, Margaret Thatcher, Jim Thorpe, and Mildred (Babe) Didrikson Zaharias, to name but a few.

As I entered adolescence, however, my feelings regarding the Apostle Paul had soured. He no longer seemed the sage and brave hero I had once thought, but in many respects a typical chauvinist. During my sophomore year in high school, I heard a sermon on Ephesians 5:22, "Wives should be subordinate to their husbands as to the Lord." Like most women in the 1970s, I took great umbrage with this. It wasn't until I audited an undergraduate course that I learned that biblical scholars consider Ephesians a deutropauline text—not actually written by Paul himself but attributed to him as one of the great teachers in order to indicate the importance of the writing, a common practice in the first century of the Common Era. This left me with much to ponder.

During my graduate studies, in a course on the Pauline writings, we studied the entire passage of Ephesians 5:21–33 and my troubled thoughts abated as we noted the reading, "Be subordinate *to one another* out of reverence for Christ" (Ephesians 5:21, emphasis added). I felt foolish for my earlier anger with Paul, and especially for not having studied the text in greater depth. I dedicated myself to studying the sacred texts and determined that I would never again allow their depth and beauty to elude me through a lack of curiosity and scholarship.

As I worked on my master's degree, I learned that the scriptural image of women in the community of faith is situated historically and culturally, and even those texts of Scripture containing stories of women were written from a predominately male perspective. The image of women and the roles of women correspond to the patriarchal culture's understanding at the time in which these sacred texts were written.[1] This primarily male perspective imbues not only the written words, stories, and histories in the Christian tradition, but also visual representations of biblical events. Paintings, sculptures, mosaics, and stained glass windows have had a greater impact than the written word in cultures where literacy was uncommon. Even in the present historical and cultural context of developed countries, in which literacy is no longer an issue, artistic depictions of religious events, stories, and persons greatly affect one's interpretation of the sacred and response to the spiritual.

In the late summer of 1980 I visited the Louvre in Paris. I vividly remember my overwhelming emotion as I saw for the first time a picture of the Madonna nursing the infant Jesus. This sixteenth-century painting shows Mary looking upon Jesus with great maternal love. This rendering of the Blessed Mother as such a feminine figure filled me with awe and wonder. Her breasts were revealed, not erotically, but rather in a nurturing and beautiful manner. I was sad and angry that the only pictures and statues of the Blessed Mother I had ever seen showed her holding the child Jesus precariously, unnaturally. In those images she had appeared flat chested and could even have been mistaken for a man if not for her veil and the lack of a beard.

During a later visit to France, I was blessed with the opportunity to visit the stunning Notre Dame de Chartres, a cathedral that serves not only as a place of worship, but also as an expression of the spirituality of the artists who so magnificently crafted the religious art that is part of the cathedral's very structure. The overwhelming beauty of the stained glass windows, sculptures, and the ancient labyrinth formed out of stones in the main body of the church speak of the human longing for the sacred. Behind the choir stalls, sculpted in stone in the thirteenth century, are more than thirty panels representing various events in the life of Christ. The expressions on the faces of the characters grace them with such fluidity and motion that they seem alive. The panel of the scene of the visitation moved me to tears as I saw for the first time an artistic representation of a visibly pregnant Mary visiting a pregnant Elizabeth.

1. Sandra M. Schneiders, *The Revelatory Text: Interpreting the New Testament as Sacred Scripture* (Collegeville, MN: Liturgical Press, 1999), 182.

During a pilgrimage to Switzerland, I went to pray at Einsiedeln Abbey Church, a Benedictine abbey more than one thousand years old. The impetus and inspiration for my pilgrimage to this holy place was Maria Anna Brunner, the foundress of my religious community, the Sisters of the Precious Blood. As I sat in the abbey church praying at the Sunday liturgy, it occurred to me that Mother Brunner, who was illiterate, came here to pray and must have found inspiration in the statue of the "Black Madonna of Einsiedeln"[2] and in the church's beautiful, lavishly painted Baroque-style ceiling. The ceiling dates from the seventeenth century and depicts important events in salvation history. These images are vibrantly colored and the characters' expressions cheerful. Some, especially the small cherubs, are even whimsical. As I pondered these picture narratives, wondering what Mother Brunner saw in this sacred art, I saw them: the women, women present even in the painted scene of the Last Supper in the dome of Einsiedeln Abbey church.

A common thread interweaves all three of these experiences with the artistic texts of the Christian faith tradition through the various historical and cultural contexts in which they were created. The sculptures I saw were fashioned in the fifteenth century and the paintings were created in the sixteenth and seventeenth centuries. In this sacred art, I witnessed women performing significant ministries during key moments of Judeo-Christian history. These images cannot be dismissed lightly as feminist hermeneutic. In this art the women are present and visible; they are part of the image text embedded in Christian history.

The inspiration for this book is two-fold then: to identify the significant ministerial role played by women in the church throughout its history, and to acknowledge the great apostle Paul for his recognition of, respect for, and inclusion of women as ministers and "co-workers" in the emerging Christian communities.

Through careful reflection on the texts of Sacred Scripture, through empathic listening, and through the creation of new and imaginative paradigms one can best engender hope. It is this hope that leads one to embrace the diversity of gifts and talents within Christian communities of faith and, like Paul, to recognize women and men as "co-workers" in announcing the Gospel of Jesus Christ.

---

2. The "Black Madonna of Einsiedeln" is a Late Gothic wooden statue from the mid-fifteenth century.

chapter 1

The Ministry of Women in the New Testament

All four Gospel accounts provide clear evidence of women disciples following and ministering to Jesus. While nowhere do the Gospel writers apply the term *mathētēs* (disciple) to any of these women of faith, arguments can be made for doing so. First, the Gospel stories recount the engagement of these women in ministries typical of "disciples" such as proclaiming the gospel, attending to the physical needs of Jesus, and going to the tomb intending to anoint the body of Jesus for burial. Secondly, biblical scholars posit that the authors of the Gospels avoided using the term *mathētēs* for these faith-filled women lest they offend the male-dominated leadership of the early Church. Although a number of the women in the stories of the Gospels are unnamed,[1] their contribution to the ministry of proclaiming the good news of Jesus Christ continues to be remembered and to inspire Christians today.

WOMEN AS MINISTERS IN THE GOSPELS

In Matthew 26:6–13 and Mark 14:3–9 the Gospel writers report the courageous and inspiring example of the unnamed woman who anoints Jesus, an action not universally approved by others with him. This woman ministers to Jesus in a way that none of the men in the story, including the host, offers to do. The beauty and significance lie in the fact that this woman responds not only to the need of the present moment, but her action foreshadows Jesus' bodily need for anointing before his burial. The unknown woman sees and responds

---

1. Examples include: Matthew 9:20–22; 15:22–28; 26:6–13; 27:56; Mark 5:25–34; 7:25–30; 14:3–9; Luke 7:12, 37–50; 8:43–48; 11:27; 13:11–12; John 4:7–42; 8:3–11; 19:25.

to a need that went unnoticed by Jesus' male disciples.[2] Jesus asks the men in the story why they criticize the woman and "make trouble" for her, or "trouble"[3] her.

Jesus emphasizes the profound significance of this woman's service to him: "Amen, I say to you, wherever this gospel is proclaimed in the whole world, what she has done will be spoken of, in memory of her" (Matthew 26:13); "Amen, I say to you, wherever the gospel is proclaimed to the whole world, what she has done will be told in memory of her" (Mark 14:9). The "memory" of this woman, her memorial, continues to be proclaimed as part of the gospel, testifying to her good deed and her greatness in the eyes of Jesus.[4]

In the Fourth Gospel, the Samaritan woman reflects the pattern of discipleship established in John 1:29–51 as she encounters Jesus, has a life-changing conversation with him, grows in her belief, and goes out to call others.[5] Jesus and the Samaritan woman enter into a lengthy and complex theological discussion, including the prophetic role of calling the people from idolatry to the worship of God "in Spirit and truth" (John 4:23). The Samaritan woman's response is a template for the apostolic formula of leaving all to follow Jesus. "The woman left her water jar and went into the town and said to the people . . . " (John 4:28). Her action parallels the stories of the male disciples in the Synoptic Gospels. Just as the men leave their boats, fishing nets, and tax stalls to follow Jesus, the Samaritan woman abandons her daily work to follow Jesus and to evangelize her town.[6] The theological discussion between Jesus and the Samaritan woman is thoughtful and reflective, and a mutual self-revelation between Jesus and the woman unfolds.[7]

---

2. Daniel J. Harrington, *The Gospel of Matthew*, Sacra Pagina, vol. 1 (Collegeville, MN: Liturgical Press, 1991), 362.

3. NRSV.

4. John R. Donahue and Daniel J. Harrington, *The Gospel of Mark*, Sacra Pagina, vol. 2 (Collegeville, MN: Liturgical Press, 2002), 368.

5. This pattern is discussed in Raymond F. Collins, *These Things Have Been Written: Studies on the Fourth Gospel* (Louvain, Belgium: Peeters Press, and Grand Rapids, MI: Eerdmans, 1990), 48–55.

6. Sandra M. Schneiders, *The Revelatory Text: Interpreting the New Testament as Sacred Scripture* (Collegeville, MN: Liturgical Press, 1999), 192.

7. Ibid., 191.

Just before the woman returns to her town and embarks upon the missionary proclamation of the Good News, the disciples arrive to find Jesus talking with the woman. The text tells us that the disciples view the scene with amazement (v. 27), and one could argue that they even disapprove of Jesus' interaction with the Samaritan woman. Using a feminist hermeneutic in approaching this text of Scripture, Sandra Schneiders asserts:

> This little interlude of the return of the disciples undoubtedly tells us more about the Johannine community than about the earthly Jesus. The theological and missionary role of the woman is profoundly unsettling to the male disciples, who see themselves as the privileged associates of Jesus, who, nevertheless, seems to have gotten along quite well without them. He does not need the food they have brought him (vv. 31–34), because his dialogue with the woman has satisfied both his hunger to do the will of the one who sent him and the thirst that symbolically mediated their encounter. And the Samaritan mission, plainly in the hands of the woman, is one in which Jesus says they will participate as "reapers." But they do not initiate it and it is not under their control (vv. 35–38). It seems not unlikely that whoever wrote the fourth gospel had some experience of women Christians as theologians and as apostles, was aware of the tension this aroused in the community, and wanted to present Jesus as legitimating female participation in male-appropriated roles.[8]

This woman went and proclaimed the Good News of Jesus Christ to her people and "many of the Samaritans of that town began to believe in him because of the word of the woman who testified" (v. 39). In all four Gospels, the Samaritan woman is the only person, male or female, who encounters Jesus and whose subsequent witness and proclamation of the word (Jesus in John's Gospel *is* the word) brings many people to "come and see" the Lord, with the result that many believed in the Lord because of her testimony.[9]

8. Schneiders, *The Revelatory Text*, 192.
9. Ibid., 193.

In addition to this unnamed women in the New Testament there are many women disciples who follow Jesus and minister to him who are identified by name. Some of them are:

Mary the mother of Jesus	Matthew 1:16, 18, 20; 2:11; 13:55; Mark 6:3; Luke 1:27, 30, 34, 38–39, 41, 46, 56; 2:5, 16, 19, 34; John 2:1, 3, 5, 12; 19:25
Mary Magdalene	Matthew 27:56, 61; 28:1; Mark 15:40, 47; 16:1, 9; Luke 8:2; 24:10; John 19:25, 20:1, 11, 16, 18
Martha	Matthew 27:56, 61; 28:1; Mark 15:40, 47; 16:1, 9; Luke 8:2; 24:10; John 19:25, 20:1, 11, 16, 18
Mary of Bethany	Luke 10:39, 42; John 11:1–2, 19–20, 28, 31–32, 45; 12:3
Mary the wife of Clopas	John 19:25
Joanna	Luke 8:3; 24:10
Mary the mother of James and Joseph	Matthew 27:56
Mary the mother of the younger James and of Joses	Mark 15:40
Joanna and Suzanna	Luke 8:3
Mary the mother of Joses	Mark 15:47
Mary the mother of James	Mark 16:1
Salome	Mark 15:40; 16:1

MARY MAGDALENE:
APOSTLE TO THE APOSTLES

The most significant woman in the New Testament, after Mary the mother of Jesus, is Mary Magdalene. The New Testament tradition, recorded in all four Gospels, presents Mary Magdalene as among the first women commissioned to proclaim the good news of the Resurrection of Jesus Christ. In the early centuries, in patristic writings and iconographic representations, Mary Magdalene is depicted as the *apostolorum apostola*, apostle to the apostles.

It is significant to note that it was the women who stayed by the cross, who anointed and prepared Jesus' body for burial, who kept vigil and mourned at the tomb, and who encountered the angel. The women also were the first to encounter and recognize the risen Christ. The absence of the male disciples in these crucial events diminishes the legacy that was extended to Peter (Matthew 16:18–19). While Jesus later forgave the male disciples for their fear, betrayal, and absence, the women were the first to be given the commission by Jesus to "go and tell" the good news of the Resurrection. Jesus affirmed the women for their faithfulness and it is through their telling of their experience at the tomb with "fear and great joy" that the essence of the Christian message—Jesus' Resurrection—was first proclaimed.[10]

In Matthew 28, an "angel of the Lord" commissions Mary Magdalene and the other women to preach the good news of Jesus' Resurrection:

> He is not here, for he has been raised just as he said. Come and see the place where he lay. Then go quickly and tell his disciples, "He has been raised from the dead, and he is going before you to Galilee; there you will see him." Behold, I have told you. (Matthew 28:6–7)

In Matthew 28:10, Jesus himself commissions these women to this task.

Mark's Gospel account also depicts Mary Magdalene and the other women's encounter with a divine messenger, described as "a

---

10. Mark Allan Powell, "Matthew," in *The HarperCollins Bible Commentary*, ed. James L. Mays (New York: HarperCollins Publishers, 2000), 899.

young man sitting on the right side, clothed in a white robe" (Mark 16:5), who says to them, "Do not be amazed! You seek Jesus of Nazareth, the crucified. He has been raised; he is not here. Behold the place where they laid him. But go and tell his disciples and Peter, 'He is going before you to Galilee; there you will see him, as he told you.'" (Mark 16:6–7)

The Gospel according to Luke describes the news of the Resurrection of Jesus being conveyed by "two men in dazzling garments" (Luke 24:4) who appear to the women, among whom Mary Magdalene is named first. These divine messengers ask Mary Magdalene and the other women (Luke 24:10),

> "Why do you seek the living one among the dead? He is not here, but he has been raised. Remember what he said to you while he was still in Galilee, that the Son of Man must be handed over to sinners and be crucified, and rise on the third day." And they remembered his words. Then they returned from the tomb and announced all these things to the eleven and to all the others. (Luke 24:5–9)

However, in Luke's version the women are not believed (Luke 24:11).

In the Gospel of John, the divine messenger is Jesus himself. Jesus chooses Mary Magdalene to be the messenger of his Resurrection and commissions her to go and tell the other disciples. The interaction between Jesus and Mary Magdalene in this Resurrection appearance is both intimate and tender. A grieving and weeping Mary recognizes Jesus when he speaks her name.

> "Mary!" She turned and said to him in Hebrew, "Rabbouni," which means Teacher. Jesus said to her, "Stop holding on to me. . . . But go to my brothers and tell them, 'I am going to my Father and your Father, to my God and your God.'" Mary of Magdala went and announced to the disciples, "I have seen the Lord," and what he told her. (John 20:16–18)

Initially, Mary Magdalene did not comprehend the message of the angel. However, after she recognized the resurrected Christ, she accepted her role as messenger and announced the words of Jesus to the other disciples.[11] Mary had an Easter experience. She moved from weak or partial faith into perfect faith and, in doing so, she did what Jesus himself commissioned her to do. She went and announced the Resurrection of Jesus. Jesus' words of commissioning to Mary Magdalene are also deeply relational, reminiscent of the words that Ruth spoke to Naomi: "Wherever you go I will go, wherever you lodge I will lodge, your people shall be my people, and your God my God" (Ruth 1:16).

Historical Misunderstanding

It is tragically ironic that even though, according to the Fourth Gospel, Mary Magdalene was the first person to encounter the resurrected Jesus and was told directly by him to preach this good news to the other disciples, today some Christian denominations would prohibit her from preaching, the very act that Jesus himself commissioned her to do.

All this raises the issue of mistaken assumptions about Mary Magdalene's character that are not borne out by Scripture. One traditional misinterpretation identifies Mary Magdalene, *apostolorum apostola*, the apostle[12] to the apostles, as a repentant prostitute. Yet nowhere in the Gospels or the entirety of the New Testament is there any reference to Mary Magdalene as a prostitute. This error has its foundation not in Scripture but in a homily given by Pope Gregory the Great on September 21, 591, in the basilica of San Clemente in Rome. Addressing the pericope in the Gospel of Luke (7:36–50) in his thirty-third homily, Pope Gregory declared, "We believe that this woman [Mary Magdalene] whom Luke calls a female sinner, whom John calls Mary, is the same Mary from whom Mark says seven demons were cast out."[13] Gregory merged a correlation among three distinct women: the unnamed woman who was a sinner (Luke 7:36–50); Mary of Bethany, sister of Martha and Lazarus (John 11:1–45; 12:1–8); and Mary Magdalene, whom Jesus healed and from whom he made seven demons depart

---

11. Francis J. Moloney, *The Gospel of John*, Sacra Pagina, vol. 4 (Collegeville, MN: Liturgical Press, 1998), 527.

12. The word *apostle* literally means "one who is sent."

13. Gregory the Great, *Homilia 33* in *Homiliarum in evangelia*, Lib. II, PL 76, 1239.

(Luke 8:2).[14] "Although Mary had 'seven demons driven from her,' the text gives us no reason to connect her to 'the sinful woman' of the previous story, although the harmonizing tendency of church tradition has done so."[15] As a result, Mary Magdalene continues to be known by many as the repentant prostitute saint. Gregory's position as pope has certainly substantiated and extended the acceptance of this distortion. The historical perspective of the ensuing fifteen centuries and advances in Scripture scholarship have provided a more accurate exegesis, however, and also an understanding of the errant exegesis of Pope Gregory. Although "penitent" was officially removed from Mary Magdalene's title by the Roman Catholic Church in 1969, popular culture and media continue to portray her as a penitent reformed prostitute.

It is important to recognize and to understand Jesus' view of women and of women as ministers as recorded in all four Gospels. Throughout the Gospel accounts of Jesus' teaching, interactions, and relationships there is not a single example of Jesus' behavior condoning the cultural and religious discrimination against women that was customary in his historical context.

INITIAL IMPRESSIONS OF PAUL'S VIEW OF WOMEN AS MINISTERS

The Acts of the Apostles gives us examples of Paul interacting with women and empowering them to function in roles of ministerial leadership in the early Christian communities. Lydia of Thyatira, mentioned in Acts 16:11–15, appears to have been prominent in Philippi's "place of prayer" (Acts 16:13). In Jewish practice a synagogue cannot form without a quorum of ten adult males. Since this gathering is not termed a synagogue, it probably was a more loosely organized gathering for prayer, without the requisite ten-man quorum. If the group consisted solely of women, Lydia may well have been their leader.

---

14. Gregory finds this last detail in Mark 16:9, which was probably not part of the original text. It is, however, found in Luke 8:2.

15. Luke Timothy Johnson, *The Gospel of Luke*, Sacra Pagina, vol. 3 (Collegeville, MN: Liturgical Press, 1991), 131.

In the Christian communities of the first century, a number of women were in positions of ministerial leadership. The undisputed letters of Paul provide unmistakable examples of women functioning as ministers within the early Church, particularly within the communities founded by Paul.

Priscilla (cf. Acts 18:2, 18, and 26), also called Prisca (cf. Romans 16:3, 1 Corinthians 16:19, and 2 Timothy 4:19), along with her husband Aquila, was the co-head of a house church. Both Prisca and Aquila accompanied Paul on one of his missionary journeys (Acts 18:18).

In the Letter to the Philippians, Paul writes about two women, Euodia and Syntyche, who "have struggled at my side in promoting the gospel" (Philippians 4:3). Paul calls these women his "co-workers," stating that their names "are in the book of life" (Philippians 4:3).

Romans 16 is replete with references to women ministers in the early Christian community. Paul acclaims a woman named Phoebe, who is a deacon: "I commend to you Phoebe our sister, who is (also) a minister[16] of the church at Cenchreae, that you may receive her in the Lord in a manner worthy of the holy ones, and help her in whatever she may need from you, for she has been a benefactor to many and to me as well" (Romans 16:1–2). Following the commendation of Phoebe, Paul sends greetings to Prisca and Aquila, emphasizing the importance of their ministry and leadership: "Greet Prisca and Aquila, my co-workers in Christ Jesus, who risked their necks for my life, to whom not only I am grateful but also all the churches of the Gentiles; greet also the church at their house" (Romans 16:3–5). The next woman named by Paul is Mary, of whom he writes: "Greet Mary, who has worked hard for you" (Romans 16:6). In the next verse Paul names another woman, Junia, as "prominent among the apostles": "Greet Andronicus and Junia, my relatives and my fellow prisoners; they are prominent among the apostles and they were in Christ before me" (Romans 16:7). Later Paul identifies three other women and recognizes their ministry: "Greet those workers in the Lord, Tryphaena and Tryphosa. Greet the beloved Persis, who has worked hard in the Lord" (Romans 16:12). The next woman remains

---

16. Although the NAB translates the Greek *diakonos* as "minister," a more accurate translation of the Greek is "deacon." The *New Greek-English Interlinear New Testament* and the NRSV both translate the Greek word *diakonos* as deacon.

unnamed; however, her status is highly significant to Paul as revealed by his words: "Greet Rufus, chosen in the Lord, and his mother and mine" (Romans 16:13). Paul concludes this "who's who" of ministerial leadership in the early Christian community, naming Julia and the sister of Nereus, "Greet Philologus, Julia, Nereus and his sister, and Olympas, and all the holy ones who are with them" (Romans 16:15).

The commendations, greetings, and words used in Paul's writings attest to the ministerial leadership of women in the early Christian churches. Paul, in his typical straightforward style, wrote courageously, audaciously revealing his feelings about women whom he regarded as apostles, co-workers, deacons, fellow prisoners, sisters, those working hard in the Lord, and holy ones. Paul listened to and responded to the concerns of women, especially as those concerns addressed the dangerous divisions that threatened the nascent Christian community at Corinth. The writings of Paul move one to ponder what might have become of the early Christian Church had Paul chosen to ignore the concerns, as well as the gifts and talents, of the women who ministered in positions of leadership in these early communities of faith. These writings are explored in detail in subsequent chapters of this book.

 ## QUESTIONS FOR DISCUSSION

1. List the various ways that the women disciples ministered to Jesus and participated in his ministry.

2. What did you learn from the stories of Mary Magdalene, Mary the mother of Jesus, the Samaritan woman, and others in the Gospels?

3. What are the leadership roles that Paul attributes to women in his writings to the early Christian communities? What is the significance of women fulfilling these roles in the early Church?

chapter 2

Paul and His Times

The first chapter provided general background about the women in the New Testament. The next three chapters explore Paul's life and cultural context, his thoughts, and his writings. The last chapter will examine the role of women in ministry from the post-New Testament Church to modernity, a role not always fully informed by the egalitarian and inclusive apostle who so often has been misunderstood and whose writings have been misappropriated regarding his attitude toward women in the Church.

THE PERSON OF PAUL

In order to have a deeper understanding and appreciation for women in the writings of Paul, it is essential to know the "messenger." Paul is one of the most compelling and intriguing figures in early Christianity. Myriad videos and books, both academic and popular, portray his travels, his passion, and his fiery personality. Contemporary thought regarding Paul's attitude toward women ranges from accusations of misogyny to accolades for daringly naming women his "co-workers" in the early Christian communities. Paul remains a complex character whose zeal and passion for spreading the good news of Jesus Christ has been, and continues to be, exemplary in the history of Christian discipleship and ministry.

The most reliable resource for Paul's life is Paul's letters (1 Thessalonians, 1 Corinthians, Philippians, Philemon, 2 Corinthians, Galatians, and Romans) are the most reliable source about his life.[1]

---

1. The letters listed here are widely agreed to have been authored by Paul. Scholars believe that the other New Testament letters that bear Paul's name were probably written by followers of Paul after his death. The list offered here is arranged in the chronological order posited by the majority of scholars, not the canonical order.

The Acts of the Apostles is a secondary source, for it was not written by Paul, and was written after his death; thus the information about Paul presented there may not be as reliable as what we find in Paul's own letters. However, the Acts of the Apostles, written by the author of the Gospel of Luke, provides many details of Paul's life, personality, and background not mentioned in Paul's letters, so Acts is a convenient place to begin.

Acts records that Paul was born a Jew, originally named Saul (Acts 9), raised in Tarsus, capital city of Cilicia in Asia Minor, now southwest Turkey (Acts 21:39 and 22:3), held Roman citizenship (Acts 22:25–28), and studied with the renowned Jewish teacher Gamaliel (Acts 22:3). At times Paul supported himself through tent making (Acts 18:3). He also was not without "human resources" to help support him in his travels. In Acts 18:11, Luke records that Paul stayed with Prisca and Aquila, to whom Paul refers several times in his letters (Romans 16:3; 1 Corinthians 16:19), for more than a year. On other occasions he stayed with Lydia, who was a dealer of purple cloth (Acts 16:14–15), and for more than a year with Titus (Acts 18:7, 11), about whom little is known.

Acts records three accounts of Paul's dramatic conversion (Acts 9:1–19; 21:37–22:21; 26:2–19). In his lengthy speech to King Agrippa in Acts 26, Paul summarizes his missionary career and describes his vision of the risen Christ.

> I myself once thought that I had to do many things against the name of Jesus the Nazorean, and I did so in Jerusalem. I imprisoned many of the holy ones with the authorization I received from the chief priests, and when they were to be put to death I cast my vote against them. Many times, in synagogue after synagogue, I punished them in an attempt to force them to blaspheme; I was so enraged against them that I pursued them even to foreign cities. On one such occasion I was traveling to Damascus with the authorization and commission of the chief priests. At midday, along the way, O king, I saw a light from the sky, brighter than the sun, shining around me and my traveling companions. We all fell to the ground and I heard a voice saying to me in Hebrew, "Saul, Saul, why are you persecuting me? It is

hard for you to kick against the goad." And I said, "Who are you, sir?" And the Lord replied, "I am Jesus whom you are persecuting. Get up now, and stand on your feet. I have appeared to you for this purpose, to anoint you as a servant and witness of what you have seen [of me] and what you will be shown. I shall deliver you from this people and from the Gentiles to whom I send you, to open their eyes that they may turn from darkness to light and from the power of Satan to God, so that they may obtain forgiveness of sins and an inheritance among those who have been consecrated by faith in me." And so, King Agrippa, I was not disobedient to the heavenly vision. (Acts 26:9–19)

Paul's letters do not describe his conversion at length as do these accounts in Acts. Nevertheless, he alludes to the event several times: "But when [God], who from my mother's womb had set me apart and called me through his grace, was pleased to reveal his Son to me, so that I might proclaim him to the Gentiles . . . " (Galatians 1:15–16) and "Last of all, as to one born abnormally, he appeared to me" (1 Corinthians 15:8).

Thus it appears that Paul was a learned and deeply devout Jew who initially opposed the Christian movement. Then he had a visionary experience that was, for him, both a revelation of Jesus as Son of God and a commission from God to proclaim the message of Jesus to Gentiles (non-Jews). It is not surprising that Paul, as a Jew, regularly adds the title "Christ" to the name Jesus; Paul wrote in Greek, and "christ" is the Greek equivalent of the Hebrew word "messiah" (both mean "anointed one"). He based much of his missionary preaching on his belief that Jesus is the fulfillment of God's promise of the Messiah as revealed in the prophetic writings of the Old Testament. Paul expresses pride and respect for his Jewish heritage in Romans 9:4–5, Galatians 1:13–14, and Philippians 3:5–6. In Philippians, Paul states that he is a Pharisee from the tribe of Benjamin who has strictly adhered to the commands of the Torah. For Paul, the faithful Jew, God is revealed in the person and ministry of Jesus, Messiah (Christ).

Much information on Paul's view of himself is found in 2 Corinthians 10–13, where he defends himself and his ministry with brutal honesty, and even sarcasm. Paul summarizes his early career as an apostle in Galatians 1:16–20 and presents his apostolic credentials in Romans 1:1–6. It is clear that Paul rests his authority as apostle upon his having been commissioned by God directly. In effect, his authority is *charismatic* (from *charism*, Greek for "gift," specifically a gift from God). It is also clear that some of the people Paul encountered questioned whether Paul's claim to authority was legitimate, since he had not been commissioned by the surviving group of Jesus' original disciples, specifically Peter, James, and John (see especially Galatians and 2 Corinthians). Paul is not anti-hierarchical: he is capable of reminding the reader that, as an apostle, he has the authority to issue commands, though he would rather persuade (Philemon 8–9). But he insists that authority for ministry ultimately comes from God. This has important implications for the way Paul handles his churches as well. Paul believes every Christian receives the Holy Spirit at baptism, and that the Spirit bestows gifts on each Christian, without exception, for ministry within the Church. The same Spirit that empowers Paul to be an apostle also empowers each member of the Church, for ministry. In chapter 4 we will see that Paul recognized a number of women as Spirit-empowered for ministry.

One must balance Paul's attributes as a well-educated man, exemplary in his missionary zeal, with an understanding of and appreciation for his spirituality and prayer. Paul's spirituality and prayer express his faith and inspire the Christian community; Christians are called to emulate him in this regard. Paul's writings make it clear that he had dedicated himself to discipleship and prayer before being a missionary or theologian. His life as a disciple illustrates his devotion to prayer and thanksgiving, which sustained his interaction with Christian converts. All of his letters begin with a greeting of thanksgiving (except the letter to the Galatians) and end with a request for and promise of prayer.[2]

Paul is no plaster saint. His humanity is evident in his letters. He feels gratitude, affection, and a nurturing tenderness: "I give thanks" (Romans 1:8; 1 Corinthians 1:4; Philippians 1:3; 1 Thessalonians 1:2 ["We"]; 2:13; and Philemon 1:4); "We were gentle among you, as a nursing mother" (1 Thessalonians 2:7); "My children, for whom I am again in labor until Christ be formed in you!" (Galatians 4:19); "Which

---

2. Gordon D. Fee, *God's Empowering Presence: The Holy Spirit in the Letters of Paul* (Peabody, MA: Hendrickson), 866.

do you prefer? Shall I come to you with a rod, or with love and a gentle spirit?" (1 Corinthians 4:21; cf. 1 Corinthians 13; Philippians 1:3–9; 2:1–4; 4:2–3). But He can also get angry and lose his patience (Galatians 3:1–3; 5:12; 1 Corinthians 14:36; 2 Corinthians 10–13).

The single most compelling thrust of Paul's life is his complete and total dedication to spreading the good news of Jesus Christ. To this end, he endured the rigors of extensive travel by sea and on foot over desert terrain; in some cities and villages he was accepted, while in others he was accosted and even imprisoned. He traveled to foreign lands, encountering harsh environments, diverse cultures, various religions, and peoples who were strange to him. In all of this Paul made the commitment to "become all things to all" (1 Corinthians 9:22) in order to share with them the good news of Jesus Christ.

PAUL'S CULTURAL CONTEXT

That phrase "all things to all" hints at the diversity Paul encountered in his missionary travels. Paul's world was far from homogeneous. Paul, a Jew born and raised in Tarsus and a Roman citizen, was immersed in a multicultural, multireligious world. His education and travels exposed him to diverse cultures, philosophies, and peoples. The philosophical, religious, social, and personal perspectives of Paul, because of his life experiences, are interwoven into a complex whole. The reality of Christ crucified and the redemption that Jesus brought about dramatically and profoundly reshaped Paul's thought, preaching, and way of living.

First-century Tarsus was not unusual in having a community of Jews living there, far from their ancestral homeland. There were Jewish communities in most cities of the Roman Empire, usually composed of merchants or tradesmen. Paul's circle of fellow-laborers for the gospel included Jewish men such as Barnabas (Acts 4:36, 9:27, 11:22, 30, 13:46, 50, 14:12, 20, 15:2, 12, 22, 25, 35–37, 39; 1 Corinthians 9:6; Galatians 2:1, 9, 13).

Most of the people Paul encountered were, nonetheless, Gentiles. In Paul's upbringing, the most fundamental distinction among human beings was that between Gentiles and Jews, for only the latter were the chosen people, entrusted with a special covenantal relationship with God. The distinction between men and women was trivial compared to that between Jews and Gentiles. From an early date, complaints were raised within the Jewish community that the followers of Jesus were blurring this all-important distinction by accepting Gentiles as full members of the Christian community; indeed, it may have been this very point that prompted Paul at first to oppose the Christians. But as a result of his conversion, Paul understood himself as called by God specifically to proclaim the gospel of Christ to Gentiles— his position had reversed completely. Most of the members of the churches Paul founded were Gentiles, and, in keeping with Paul's principle that all who receive Christ are endowed by the Holy Spirit with gifts for ministry, we find a number of Gentiles in positions of prominence in those churches. They include Titus (2 Corinthians 2:13, 7:6, 13–14, 8:6, 16, 23, 12:18; Galatians 2:1, 3) and Timothy (Acts 16:1, 17:14–15, 18:5, 19:22, 20:4; Romans 16:21; 1 Corinthians 4:17, 16:10; 2 Corinthians 1:1, 19; Philippians 1:1, 2:19; 1 Thessalonians 1:1, 3:1–2, 6).

The members of Paul's congregations came from all walks of life. Some were obviously well off, for they owned houses large enough to accommodate the early Christian congregations gathered for worship (Romans 16:5; 1 Corinthians 16:19; Philemon 2). Most were at the lower end of society, including a number of slaves (1 Corinthians1:26). One of these, Onesimus, figures prominently in Paul's letter to Philemon (Philemon 10–11). Paul is sometimes faulted for his failure to condemn the institution of slavery. The fact is, Paul was a man of his time, and it seems never to have occurred to him that there could be a world without masters and slaves. Nevertheless, Paul insists that in Christ new realities have come into existence, realities that transcend the existing order of society. He calls upon Philemon to recognize a slave, Onesimus, as his brother (Philemon 16). In effect, the new, Christian, realities have relativized the social structure so as to negate it almost completely. Non-Christians saw such disregard for traditional hierarchical relationships as shocking and subversive to the very fabric of society. Not surprisingly, Paul was accused of "turning the world upside down" (Acts 17:6 NRSV).

In much the same way, Paul is a man of his day with regard to the family. In Greco-Roman society, the family was the most basic and, in many ways, most important institution. Whereas the modern democratic system is centered on the individual, both in regard to personal rights and freedom, the Roman view held that the basic organizational structure of government was founded upon the family, headed by a *paterfamilias*. Relationships were elaborately ordered and extremely hierarchical, rooted in reason. The prevailing philosophies taught that men have the highest form of reason, women possess reason to a much less developed extent, and children possess the potential to develop reason. Family hierarchy was essential because the Romans used it to legitimate and justify their dominance over all other people.[3]

Paul seems never to have imagined that a household could be organized any other way than that with which he was familiar; at one point he actually refers to the husband as the wife's "head" (1 Corinthians 11:3). But here too he sees the new realities in Christ superseding existing social structures. He insists that, before God, there is a reciprocity between husband and wife, a mutuality of respect and responsibility (1 Corinthians 7:3–4; 11:11–12) that would have sounded shocking and subversive in his day. Because the patriarchal family undergirded the social and political structure in the Roman world, any ideology or praxis that challenged or threatened the hierarchical structure of the family was perceived as an imminent danger to the Roman Empire. In light of this, one can see why any patriotic Roman citizen would object to Paul's assertion, in his letter to the Galatians, that in Christ the differences between Jews and Greeks, slaves and free persons, and men and women (3:28), have been abolished. Such countercultural views undermined the fundamental structures of society, and ultimately threatened the rationale by which Rome and its citizens justified domination of the first-century Mediterranean world. Christians who held such views would have been liable to a charge of treason.[4]

Paul's writings show that his understanding of the Christian community is intimately interconnected with the workings of the Holy Spirit,[5] as he views the diversity and unity in the community as Spirit-filled. For Paul, the manifestations of the Spirit are witnessed in the charisms of each believer in the communities of faith (1 Corinthians 12). Paul clearly exhorts the Christian community to remember

---

3. Ibid., 288.
4. Ibid.
5. 1 Corinthians 12:4–11; 2 Corinthians 1:22; 3:3, 6, 8, 17–18; 5:5; Philippians 1:19; 2:1; 3:3.

that diversity, not uniformity, is essential for a healthy church, that the one God who is characterized by diversity within unity has decreed the same for the Church.[6] Moreover, Paul recognizes that God does not give such charisms to men only. Women, too, receive such gifts of the Holy Spirit, including the gift of prophecy (1 Corinthians 11:5), which Paul prizes as the foremost of the spiritual gifts because of its usefulness in the ministry of the Church (1 Corinthians 14:1–5). Paul was particularly close to a husband and wife team, Prisca and Aquila (Acts 18:2, 18; 1 Corinthians 16:19; Romans 16:3); there is good reason to believe that Prisca was the dominant member of this ministry team, not her husband Aquila. A number of single women also appear, such as Euodia and Syntyche (Philippians 4:2–3) and Phoebe (Romans 16:1). Such examples will be examined in detail in chapter 4.

RELIGION AND PHILOSOPHY

The modern prevailing worldview is almost a polar opposite of that of Paul's era. The predominant worldview today highly touts the latest technological advances, whatever is "new and improved." The Mediterranean world in the first century CE was quite different. What was old was considered to be of great value, and new or recent ideas were suspect.[7] For the people of the first century, the present was not an age of enlightenment or improvement, but rather a direct link to the treasures of past wisdom. Ancestors were considered noble and were held in high esteem. Because of this suspicion of things new, if Christianity had proclaimed itself a "new religion" it would have been met, at best, with suspicion and, at worst, with absolute rejection.[8] In the Roman Empire, it was understood that all cultures and nations had their own traditional gods, goddesses, and religious practices. Rome did not interfere with the religious practices of those it conquered or who were otherwise part of their empire, unless the "foreign religion" or its practices were thought to encourage rebellion against Rome and its dominance.[9] The Christian communities of

---

6. Fee, *God's Empowering Presence*, 159.

7. Paul J. Achtmemeier, Joel B. Green, and Marianne Meye Thompson, *Introducing the New Testament: Its Literature and Theology* (Grand Rapids: Eerdmans, 2001), 284.

8. Ibid.

9. Ibid., 285.

Paul's time were tolerated because Rome regarded them as members of a Jewish sect. However, when the followers of Jesus separated from Judaism, Christianity did not look like a legitimate religion, because it no longer appeared to be the traditional beliefs and practices of a particular ethnic group: the only thing that all members of the Christian community had in common was their faith in and allegiance to Christ. Religion was an essential part of public life, and it would have been unthinkable for any public activity not to include a religious dimension.[10] All public activity of the first century included prayer and worship of local gods and goddesses. Christians were reluctant to participate in these normative social activities, resulting in their persecution.[11] A further obstacle to early Christians was the fact that in Greco-Roman culture members of a household were not permitted to engage in religious practices not approved by their *paterfamilias*. Consequently, for a woman, child, or slave to practice Christianity in defiance of the will of the *paterfamilias* was perceived as highly subversive to the good order of the family.

Paul used Greek philosophy and thought in order to connect with Gentiles. In fact, Christianity, like Judaism, had more in common with Greco-Roman philosophy than Greco-Roman religion. Religion was concerned primarily with performing the rites required by the gods: it was a civic duty, even a patriotic duty, but had little to do with the way people lived their daily lives. Philosophy was more interested in a comprehensive system of belief that had a bearing upon every aspect of life. One major difference between philosophy and Christianity was that, among the Greeks and Romans, philosophy was almost exclusively limited to men, primarily because it was widely assumed that women lacked the requisite intellectual capacity. In contrast, women play an active role in the Pauline churches (see chapter 4).

Paul understood flesh (*sarx*) and spirit (*pneuma*) in much the same way as his philosophically-minded contemporaries. However, Paul focused on the individual's relationship to God and to the community of faith. Paul asserted that the sinfulness of the human person was rooted in the arrogance of autonomy, which results in a rupture in relationship due to a loss of the understanding of interconnectedness.

---

10. Ibid., 286.

11. Ibid., 286–87.

A person is justified before God, according to Paul, by the utterly gratuitous mercy of God. Therefore, flesh and spirit are not merely philosophical constructs (the component parts of a human being) but, in fact, alternate ways of relating to others and to God.[12] For Paul, living according to the flesh means putting oneself ahead of all others, God included, resulting in disrupted relationships; living according to the spirit means acknowledging one's human sinfulness and depending upon God's grace, mending one's severed relationship with God and others.

Paul's emphasis on relationship is embedded in the individual's belonging to Christ and, by extension, to the Christian community of faith. The driving force in Paul's personal life, as well his experience of social interactions and commitment in relationships, is focused on the dying and rising of Christ. For Paul the struggle inherent in every human life was a common experience that was deeply personal and relational, not merely academic. Paul radically challenged the arrogant and prevailing intellectual understanding of his day and instead asserted the prominence of love over precision and conformity.[13]

Paul was experienced in the Roman philosophical and intellectual understanding as well as the variety of social norms of his time. He understood the perception of the majority, which held the importance of reason and nature, the mystery surrounding the gods and goddesses, the expectations for religious worship, and the idealism of moral rhetoric.[14] Influenced by these varied perspectives, Paul acquiesced to the prevailing view of his day in some areas, while at other times, he was critical and original in his teaching. His thinking and preaching were creative, especially his foundational focus on the revelation of God in Christ Jesus and in the Spirit. Paul did not argue for reason against faith, and challenged the arrogant intellectualism of the majority (1 Corinthians 4:18–21).[15]

As a consummate missionary, Paul could reach out to and connect with dissimilar people precisely because he was adaptable, flexible, and willing to accommodate the needs of others. Christ's gospel,

---

12. Mark Strom, *Reframing Paul: Conversations in Grace and Community* (Downers Grove, IL: InterVarsity Press, 2000), 94.

13. Ibid., 113.

14. Ibid., 104.

15. Ibid., 110.

the message of the cross and Resurrection of Jesus Christ, motivated Paul's willingness to become "all things to all":

> Although I am free in regard to all, I have made myself a slave to all so as to win over as many as possible. To the Jews I became like a Jew to win over Jews; to those under the law I became like one under the law—though I myself am not under the law—to win over those under the law. To those outside the law I became like one outside the law—though I am not outside God's law but within the law of Christ—to win over those outside the law. To the weak I became weak, to win over the weak. I have become all things to all, to save at least some.
>
> All this I do for the sake of the gospel, so that I too may have a share in it. (1 Corinthians 9:19–23)

Paul expresses his purpose in utilizing this pastoral approach as to "save" and "win" others "for the sake of the gospel." He encourages those in the community to act responsibly and nurture the one body of Christ.[16] His belief that the end of time would occur in his lifetime, a belief commonly held in the early Christian community, encouraged his sense of urgency. Paul felt compelled to win as many converts as possible before the return of the resurrected Christ.

LEGACY AND INFLUENCE

The fervent missionary ministry of Paul was essential to the survival of the nascent Christian community of the first century. Paul wrote many of his letters to address crises that threatened the unity and life of the fledgling communities of faith. He established his authority by insisting that his position was equal to that of the other apostles based upon his vision of the resurrected Christ (Galatians 1:11–12, 15–17).

In order to appreciate the intensity of Paul's zeal for preaching the gospel of Jesus Christ, it is imperative to recognize that Paul anticipated and fully expected to experience the *parousia*, Christ's return in glory, in his lifetime (1 Thessalonians 4:15–17). It is precisely because of this expectation that Paul found societal and

---

16. James D. G. Dunn, *The Theology of Paul the Apostle* (Grand Rapids: Eerdmans, 1998), 576–77.

religious issues such as slavery (e.g. Onesimus in Philemon) and the equality of women in society secondary to preaching the gospel. The urgency of Paul's travels, the intensity of his emotions, and the passion of his writing were founded in his belief that the eschatological reign of God was imminent. This divine imperative to preach the gospel of Jesus consumed Paul because he was utterly convinced that God had achieved salvation for the world in the person and mission of Jesus Christ. For Paul, Jesus Christ is the glory of God the Father who graces his followers with the Holy Spirit and who utterly changes the relationship between God and humanity. In Jesus Christ, suffering, sin, and death have been overcome. For Paul, God's utterly gratuitous love and compassion (*xaris*, which corresponds to the Hebrew *hesed*) grace all humanity, Jew and Greek, slave and free, male and female, with freedom from the law and with salvation in Christ.

The impact of Paul and his ministry in the early Church is unmistakably documented in his own writings, in the Acts of the Apostles, and in the disputed Pauline letters that are attributed to his authorship and extol his example as a model pastor. Paul's missionary journeys provided him with the challenge of communicating the gospel message to peoples of diverse cultural and religious milieus. Significantly, Paul's words of praise, admiration, thanksgiving, admonition, and challenge, addressed to the early Christian communities of the first century CE, are equally relevant and applicable for Christians today.

QUESTIONS FOR DISCUSSION

1. What can we learn from the three accounts (Acts 9:1–19, 21:37–22:21, 26:2–19) of Paul's conversion and life as an apostle?

2. Discuss Paul's emphasis on unity in the Body of Christ. How does this emphasis on unity impact the discussion regarding issues that divide, both within and among, Christian denominations today?

3. Discuss the cultural context of Paul's time. Compare and contrast those cultures with cultures today.

4. In what ways does Paul share the opinions of his contemporaries? Give examples of ways that Paul counters the prevailing views of his day.

chapter 3

Paul's Theology of Baptism

Paul's theology of baptism provides critical insight into his writings and emphasis on equality in Christ, which is the Christian basis for equal treatment of women. Paul's first-century theology and experience of baptism, which shaped the understanding of the early Christian communities of faith, were far different from that of sacramental baptism as celebrated in twenty-first-century Christianity. Paul understood his primary mission was to preach the gospel of Jesus Christ. For him baptism was evangelistic, a ritual celebration of initiation for new adult believers into the Christian community, rather than pastoral, a ritual celebration of welcoming infants into the faith community.[1] Baptism was not an end in itself, but part of the complex whole of initiation into the Christian community. Paul does not often speak explicitly of baptism, but rather alludes to it through metaphors such as washing, anointing, sealing, putting on clothes, all of which were first-century images of baptism.[2]

BAPTISM: A BEGINNING

In the first century, baptism alone was not enough for full membership in the Christian community, but just the beginning of a commitment to a fully integrated life as a Christian. Paul identifies three main aspects of this integrated life: justification by faith, becoming one with Christ, and sharing in the life of the Holy Spirit.[3] The integration of these aspects and the consequent responsibilities

---

1. James D. G. Dunn, *The Theology of Paul the Apostle* (Grand Rapids: Eerdmans, 1998), 457.

2. Ibid., 443.

3. Ibid., 442.

expected in the life of a Christian, in Paul's vision, involved a lifelong commitment.

As Paul journeyed among the early Christian communities preaching and evangelizing, many people heard him, were inspired by the gospel he preached, and were baptized. There is neither explicit nor implicit reference to preparation for baptism in the Pauline communities or in the accounts in the Acts of the Apostles. It is understood that there was a tradition of handing on the faith and of instructing new converts. In the early Christian communities of faith, baptism was the first response of conversion, ritualizing the believer's commitment to God's invitation to share in the life of the Holy Spirit.[4]

In Paul's theology of baptism, the activity of the Spirit graces the Christian to live by faith, and calls forth and empowers the believer's conversion. This entails a commitment to a life of embracing the Spirit totally and, through prayerful discernment, being led by the Spirit.[5] "Do you not know that you are the temple of God, and that the Spirit of God dwells in you?" (1 Corinthians 3:16) As Paul addresses the early Christian communities, he calls for unity and for honoring of the gifts of the Spirit. Such gifts are given to whomever the Spirit wishes, without distinction, because the Spirit gives gifts for the common good, not for prestige, power, or control. Instead, the validity of the gifts of the Spirit is rooted in the graciousness of God: "But one and the same Spirit produces all of these, distributing them individually to each person as he wishes" (1 Corinthians 12:11). For Paul, one's experience of conversion is intertwined with the action of the Spirit in one's life.[6] In his view, the power of the Spirit at work in the lives of the early Christians was more essential to their conversion and initiation experience than the ritual action of baptism.[7]

According to Paul, every person graced by faith and endowed with the gifts of the Spirit becomes sacred because she or he has "been purchased at a price" (1 Corinthians 7:23), redeemed by the precious blood of Jesus Christ. In accepting faith and in embarking upon the Christian journey, the Christian is no longer her own or his own, but is now in

---

4. Gordon D. Fee, *God's Empowering Presence: The Holy Spirit in the Letters of Paul* (Peabody, MA: Hendrickson, 1994), 860.

5. Ibid., 864–65.

6. Ibid., 855.

7. Dunn, *The Theology of Paul the Apostle*, 453.

Christ and belongs to Christ. Likewise, the gifts do not belong to any individual; they are bestowed by the Spirit and belong to the Spirit. In Paul's view, the Spirit stamps the Christian with the seal of new ownership and makes it clear that she or he now belongs to God.[8]

In discussing Paul's theology of baptism, it is imperative to include all of these elements that Paul believed were crucial to salvation: justification by faith, participation in Christ, and the gift of the Spirit. Paul emphasized different elements depending on the community he was addressing, but his theology is comprehensive and consistent taken as a whole.

BAPTISMAL FORMULAS

Many scripture scholars find in 1 Corinthians 12:13 and Galatians 3:27–28 evidence of a baptismal formula established in the early Christian communities. Paul draws upon this formula when he calls upon the communities to put aside differences, racial and socio-economic divisions, and in Galatians, gender divisions. He calls upon the communities to recognize and to honor their unity in Christ, a unity into which each person is baptized. These passages address both the pain of exclusion and the hope of unity in the Body of Christ. Inherent in this Pauline baptismal formula is the fundamental equality of all of the baptized, including their call to ministry and their sharing in the gifts from the Holy Spirit.

The baptismal formula in First Corinthians reads: "As a body is one though it has many parts, and all the parts of the body, though many, are one body, so also Christ. For in one Spirit we were all baptized into one body, whether Jews or Greeks, slaves or free persons, and we were all given to drink of one Spirit." (1 Corinthians 12:12–13)

Ancient literature commonly employed the image of the human body to symbolize unity. This metaphor, as articulated in the writings of Aesop, Plato, and Cicero,[9] would have been familiar to Paul, who was probably educated in the classics. Paul appropriates this metaphor differently, however. His exhortations are not from a political, social, or philosophical perspective, but rather from a new theological

---

8. Ibid.

9. Further information is provided in Raymond Collins, *First Corinthians*, Sacra Pagina 7, (Collegeville, MN: Liturgical Press, 1999), 458–59.

perspective. Paul insists that the unity in diversity exhibited in the human body comes from God (1 Corinthians 12:18, 24).[10] He proceeds to call for the abolition of situations that subjugate one Christian to another. For example, Paul urges the Christian community at Corinth to live as the members of one body, recognizing the essential role of each person and the varying gifts bestowed by the Spirit, with no distinction or discrimination. Further, in calling for unity, Paul exhorts the community to honor diversity and to utilize their gifts for the common good (1 Corinthians 12:7; cf. Romans 12:3–8). Paul expresses the ideal of interdependence (1 Corinthians 12:21, 25–26) and equality rather than subordination.[11]

Paul uses a baptismal formula in 1 Corinthians 12:13 when he reminds the community that "in one Spirit we were all baptized into one body." In this formula, Paul equates the power of the Spirit at work in baptism and incorporation into the Body of Christ.[12] He continues, "whether Jews or Greeks, slaves or free persons," here exhorting the community to become one body in Christ and urging them to relinquish positions of privilege and to abolish all barriers that inhibit this unity. For Paul, this baptismal unity transcends ethnic and social differences and is the very foundation of life in the Christian community, because being in Christ is the very reason for which the community exists. When the Christian is in Christ, all differences are eliminated.

In Galatians, Paul extends the case for eradication of differences under Christ to include gender: "For all of you who were baptized into Christ have clothed yourselves with Christ. There is neither Jew nor Greek, there is neither slave nor free person, there is not male and female; for you are all one in Christ Jesus." (Galatians 3:27–28) In Galatians 3:28, the reference to the gender distinction that is transcended in baptism reflects the first account of the story of creation (Genesis 1:27). Perhaps Paul omitted the reference "not male and female" from 1 Corinthians 12:13 because of the lack of understanding among the Corinthians regarding the nature of human sexuality and their being "in Christ."[13]

---

10. Ibid., 460.

11. Ibid.

12. Ibid., 463.

13. Ibid.

Another baptismal metaphor that Paul uses in his writings, particularly in Romans, 1 Corinthians, and Galatians, is that of clothing: "to put on Christ." In Galatians 3:27–28 Paul employs this metaphor, exhorting Christians, both in antiquity and in the third millennium, as an expression of faith, to put on Christ, to become as Christ. For Paul and the Christians of the first century this action is initially expressed in baptism. Paul regards baptism as the moment when Christ, like a garment, envelops the believer.[14] Paul's use of the metaphor of "putting on Christ" is rooted in the baptismal practices of the early centuries. In these rituals, the newly baptized women and men literally removed their old clothes and, after emerging from the water, put on identical new garments. This action symbolized that they, indeed, were now new persons and one in Christ.[15]

Paul exhorts the community of believers at Galatia to focus on their unity and oneness in Christ. All of the designations that the world employs to divide people are now abolished in Christ. Baptism, unlike circumcision, is open to everyone. Old distinctions of gender (1 Corinthians 11:2–16; 14:34–35), religion (Romans 3:22–23; 10:12), and social position (1 Corinthians 7:22; Philemon 16) are of no consequence in the body of Christ. In their new identity in Christ, all of the baptized become one.[16]

Because baptism is offered to all who are in Christ, Paul's plea for unity is not merely a platitude. Paul recognized that disunity threatened the survival of the nascent Christian churches and that, if the community of the faithful did not respond to his admonition, the demise of Christianity was imminent. One can apply Paul's understanding and admonition for unity to the Church today. Perhaps the declining number of both clergy and faithful reflects a lack of openness to the Holy Spirit, resulting in the sad divisions among Christians today, keeping them from being fully in Christ. The unity of Christians from the first to the twenty-first centuries is rooted in

14. Frank Matera, *Galatians*, Sacra Pagina 9 (Collegeville, MN: Liturgical Press, 1992), 145.

15. Kristen Plinke Bentley and Sharyn Dowd, "Galatians," in *The IVP Women's Bible Commentary*, ed. Catherine Clark Kroeger and Mary J. Evans (Downers Grove, IL: InterVarsity, 2002), 685–86. See also Wayne A. Meeks, *The First Urban Christians: The Social World of the Apostle Paul* (New Haven: Yale University Press, 1983), 151.

16. William Baird, "Galatians," in *The HarperCollins Bible Commentary*, ed. James L. Mays (New York: HarperCollins, 2000), 1109.

the person of Jesus Christ, in whom all religious, social, political, and sexual/gender discrimination must cease. Anything that divides and diminishes the unity of the community of faith, thereby threatening the life of the Church, is a desecration of the Christ in whom all Christians have been baptized and thus have become one.

The words "no longer male and female" make clear that Paul intends believers to understand the necessity of including both male and female as children of God. In Paul's time all inheritances were handed down from father to son. However, in this new community of faith, mothers and daughters too inherit the promises of Christ.[17]

The believer's being in Christ, and therefore incorporated into Christ, necessarily effects a change in the present and assures that the fullness of that change will be effected in the Second Coming. Faith is initiated and made possible through the power of the Holy Spirit so that believers inherit the promises of God by the saving actions of Jesus Christ. Baptism is a profession of this faith and identification with Christ into whom the believer has become incorporated.[18] Those who believe in Christ Jesus are called to be formed into new eschatological persons. As such, they cannot deny another person full access to God's people, for God is impartial.[19] Discrimination, division, and prejudice, regardless of their foundation, diminish the presence of Christ and thus weaken and harm the community of faith. Believers have become a new creation in Christ and the old divisions of race, class, and sex have been eradicated.[20]

FREEDOM IN CHRIST

Paul reminds the Christian communities that their freedom in Christ is a gift from God for all believers, both men and women, and that a hallmark of this freedom is unity. He speaks of Christians as having been "purchased at a price" (1 Corinthians 6:20; 7:23).[21] Paul instructs Christians that freedom is not free, but is nonetheless

---

17. Ibid.

18. Matera, *Galatians*, 146.

19. Ibid., 147.

20. Ibid., 146.

21. Joseph A. Fitzmyer, "Pauline Theology," in *The New Jerome Biblical Commentary*, ed. Raymond E. Brown, Joseph A. Fitzmyer, and Roland E. Murphy (Englewood Cliffs, NJ: Prentice Hall, 1990), 1400.

a sacred gift that cannot be purchased or earned by human beings. It is an utterly gratuitous gift of God incarnate in the person of Jesus, who graced humanity with the outpouring of his precious blood. The freedom in Christ in which Paul urges the community in Corinth to live is also a call to mutuality. In Christian mutuality, both freeborn and slave, Jews and Greeks, women and men are equals in the community of faith because they are in Christ and have one Lord.[22]

In 1 Corinthians 10:14–33 Paul raises the issue of freedom of conscience. He addresses both those who believe they are still bound by the law and those who believe that they have been freed from the law because of their freedom in Christ. Paul writes that these matters of conscience, however significant, are secondary to concern for others and for the building up of the community of faith. While Paul expresses the importance of freedom in Christ ("all things are lawful"), he also explains that everything lawful does not necessarily benefit the community.[23] For Christians, merely following the law cannot be the sole basis for action. Paul argues, "'Everything is lawful,' but not everything is beneficial. 'Everything is lawful,' but not everything builds up." (1 Corinthians 10:23)

Paul exhorts believers to make unity and the building up of the faith community, the body of Christ, the primary motivation and guiding principle for their actions rather than focusing on mere laws. Christ has abolished the old laws regarding clean and unclean foods (Romans 10:4), for example. What one eats is irrelevant. Love is now the guiding principle over all things. Paul teaches believers that observing the law is secondary; charity is of primary importance in matters of conscience.[24] Christian freedom must be exercised in love.

In 2 Corinthians 3:17 the life-giving Spirit of whom Paul speaks is the Spirit of the Lord Jesus Christ, and equally the Spirit of the living God. This Spirit brings the Christian freedom from adherence to the letter of the law. Spirit, a feminine word both in Hebrew (*ruah*) and in Greek (*pneuma*), means breath. The Spirit of the Lord is breath of life, breath of God, and divine giver of life.

---

22. Elisabeth Schüssler Fiorenza, "1 Corinthians," in *The HarperCollins Bible Commentary*, ed. James L. Mays (New York: HarperCollins Publishers, 2000), 1083.

23. Mary Ann Getty, "1 Corinthians," in *The Collegeville Bible Commentary*, ed. Robert J. Karris (Collegeville, MN: Liturgical Press, 1992), 1120.

24. Ibid.

Married or Unmarried, One in Christ

Paul illustrates another aspect of freedom in Christ in his advice to virgins and widows in 1 Corinthians 7:25–28. The core of this section is Paul's advice to the unmarried.[25] "Now in regard to virgins I have no commandment from the Lord, but I give my opinion as one who by the Lord's mercy is trustworthy. So this is what I think best because of the present distress: that it is a good thing for a person to remain as he is. Are you bound to a wife? Do not seek a separation. Are you free of a wife? Then do not look for a wife. If you marry, however, you do not sin, nor does an unmarried woman sin if she marries: but such people will experience affliction in their earthly life, and I would like to spare you that." (1 Corinthians 7:25–28) These verses are open to misinterpretation unless set in their historical context. Paul offers advice to a Christian community whose members expect an imminent eschaton. Their concerns regarding eschatological existence created tension in the community. Paul argues that both men and women have the right to remain single, and recommends that they do so, because he believes Christ's return is imminent. Paul highlights his understanding of men and women as equal by saying precisely the same thing to both.[26] In Paul's view, the primary loyalty of a Christian disciple is to Christ, and for Paul freedom from the obligation of marriage enhanced each person's ability to serve Christ and the Christian community without encumbrance. Foremost in Paul's reasoning regarding the preference for the unmarried state is his conviction that the end of time, the *parousia*, is imminent.[27]

In Greco-Roman culture of the first century CE, various philosophical traditions (Gnosticism, Stoicism, and all forms of asceticism) esteemed chastity for men as an expression of self-control. However, in a society in which marriage was the customary fate of daughters and which viewed a woman's sexual morality as a sign of the health of household, city, and state, a celibate woman threatened

---

25. Collins, *First Corinthians*, 288.

26. Jerome Murphy-O'Connor, "The First Letter to the Corinthians," in *The New Jerome Biblical Commentary*, ed. Raymond E. Brown, Joseph A. Fitzmyer, and Roland E. Murphy (Englewood Cliffs, NJ: Prentice Hall, 1990), 805.

27. Dunn, *The Theology of Paul the Apostle*, 693.

the cultural norm and elicited suspicion.[28] Paul's affirmation of the right of a woman to choose celibacy is therefore counter-cultural. Paul addresses married couples and offers advice regarding celibacy in 1 Corinthians 7: 1–7 and 7:10, illustrating that when one is truly free in Christ, whether married or celibate, one can follow the baptismal calling.

Paul's belief in the imminence of the *parousia* profoundly affected his focus on preaching the good news of Jesus Christ. Paul's primary goal was neither to ratify nor change the institutions of his day. Rather, his burning passion and desire was to proclaim Christ and Christ crucified.

Nonetheless Paul is quite clear in addressing the negative effect of the social stratifications and distinctions (Jew or Greek, slave or free, male or female) within the Christian community. The threefold repetition within Paul's writing may well be viewed as a fitting conclusion to the rejection of the status quo related to the social distinctions of gender (7:1–16), ethnicity (7:18–19), and social status (7:21–23).[29] All are one by virtue of common baptism into Christ.

Slave or Master, One in Christ

The ultimate importance of Paul's Letter to Philemon lies in its enduring and powerful message of how Christians are to treat one another in Christ. Paul addresses the relationship between Onesimus and Philemon as that of slave to master. However, now that both are in Christ as baptized Christians, from Paul's perspective, they have become related to one another in a profound manner that transcends even death.

Paul exhorts Philemon to treat Onesimus no longer as his inferior, which is his social and legal right (and duty) as master. Rather, because of their equal status in Christ, Philemon ought not only treat Onesimus as an equal, but also embrace him as a brother in Christ. Paul's letter questions how masters and slaves are to treat one another in the community of faith. He gives no explicit answer, but

---

28. Margaret Y. MacDonald, "Reading Real Women Through the Undisputed Letters of Paul," in *Women and Christian Origins*, ed. Ross Shepard Kraemer and Mary Rose D'Angelo (New York: Oxford University Press, 1999), 213.

29. Collins, *First Corinthians*, 276.

rather presents a plea based on baptism and calls for Christians to answer these questions of relationship. Paul's persuasive argument points to a more basic question regarding the position of master and subordinate not only in the community of faith, but also in society. Paul pleads with Philemon to accept Onesimus as he would receive Paul himself, his partner (v. 17), fellow worker (v. 1), and brother (vv. 7, 20).[30]

The institution of slavery is abhorrent by most modern standards, but it was unquestioned in the first century CE. Again, it is important to remember that for Paul the imminence of the *parousia* necessitated spreading the good news rather than working for systemic change. Paul focuses on the needs of the emerging Church rather than on the abolition of unjust practices such as slavery. While a cursory reading of the text might move one to question Paul's emphasis, it is important to recall Paul's zeal and passion for spreading the good news to the early Church. How Philemon receives Onesimus is rooted in the very core of what it means to be baptized in Christ. If Onesimus is not recognized and received as a brother in Christ, then the belief that every Christian becomes a child of God at baptism is threatened.

Paul demonstrates to Philemon, and to the house church that gathered in Philemon and Apphia's home, the unity in Christ to which Christians are called. Paul urges Philemon to recognize that the response he makes as a Christian requires him to reject conventional practices and laws. Christians have been given a new command and a new order to live through baptism into Christ.[31]

A New Creation in Christ

In his letters Paul does not concentrate on the familial designations of siblings but rather on the identity of believers as brothers and sisters because they have become children of God through baptism (cf. Romans 8:12–17; Galatians 3:26–4:7). Baptism transforms believers into brothers and sisters in the present. This relationship

---

30. Norman R. Petersen, "Philemon," in *The HarperCollins Bible Commentary*, ed. James L. Mays (New York: HarperCollins Publishers, 2000), 1146.

31. Ivan Havener, "Philemon," in *The Collegeville Bible Commentary*, ed. Robert J. Karris (Collegeville, MN: Liturgical Press, 1992), 1171.

will be realized fully in the end times, in the kingdom of God.[32] If one does not relate to a brother or a sister in Christ as an equal, one's status as a child of God is in jeopardy, both in the Church and, therefore, also in the kingdom of God.[33]

In 2 Corinthians 5:17 Paul affirms that the individual Christian, as well as the entire community of faith, is a new creation in Christ. The tragic divisions of male and female, slave and free, Jew and Gentile, which harm and threaten to destroy the Christian community, are viewed as "old things," no longer relevant to those who are in Christ. As a new creation in Christ, the Christian community is called to an essential conversion in its relationships with all who are in Christ. Baptism effects a radical transformation in each believer to such an extent that those who are "in Christ" participate in the new creation (v. 17). The impetus for this transformation is the utterly gratuitous love of Christ expressed through the cross, which directs the actions of every believer (v. 14; cf. Galatians 6:14–15).[34]

This new creation in Christ is relevant to the Church today because all who are in Christ are called to participate in the mission of the reconciling love of God at work in the world. Further, believers are called to reach out beyond human designations that divide such as gender, race, ethnicity, nationality, and economic position to unification of all who are in Christ. This rebirth in Christ calls believers into the divine work of reconciliation. Authentic reconciliation is not a matter of legislation or law but calls the believer beyond "hardness of heart" into the transforming love of Christ. Christ, who through his love reconciled believers to God, calls them to be reconcilers. The arduous work of reconciliation calls the believer not to speak on his or her own behalf, but rather on behalf of Christ.[35]

Created anew in Christ (Galatians 6:15), each individual in the Christian community, not merely those who have been ordained or who are in positions of institutional leadership, has been sent out

---

32. Petersen, "Philemon," 1147.

33. Ibid.

34. Victor Paul Furnish, "2 Corinthians," in *The HarperCollins Bible Commentary*, ed. James L. Mays (New York: HarperCollins Publishers, 2000), 1098.

35. Sandra Hack Polaski, "2 Corinthians," in *The IVP Women's Bible Commentary*, ed. Catherine Clark Kroeger and Mary J. Evans (Downers Grove, IL: InterVarsity, 2002), 670.

into the world to share the message of God's reconciling love. The God of the Genesis creation accounts (Genesis 1:1–31 and 2:4b–25), who formed the earth out of nothing, can transform and endow the individual with the gifts and talents to share in this divine work. Not only the apostles, but all believers who are in Christ are empowered and sent to share in the work of reconciliation.[36]

Tragically, even though the call to preach the message of divine reconciliation has been given to all who are in Christ, human beings who feel that their power, privilege, and control might be threatened by this radical new creation continue to avoid this exhortation from Paul. Change is usually met with resistance and "new things" only survive if there is human acceptance.[37] Ultimately, radical change occurs through the lived acceptance of the standard of humanity represented by Christ.[38] As the following chapter will demonstrate, Paul's attitude toward women reflects his view of equality in Christ resulting from baptism and conversion.

QUESTIONS FOR DISCUSSION

1. Summarize Paul's theology of baptism.

2. Discuss Paul's understanding of the gifts of the Spirit given to the Christian community.

3. In what way, if any, have you experienced discrimination in your life?

4. What are the similarities and the differences in the experiences of a faith community today as contrasted with the faith communities of Paul?

---

36. Mary Ann Getty, "2 Corinthians," in *The Collegeville Bible Commentary*, ed. Robert J. Karris (Collegeville, MN: Liturgical Press, 1992), 1142.

37. Jan Lambrecht, *Second Corinthians*, Sacra Pagina 8 (Collegeville, MN: Liturgical Press, 1999), 97.

38. Jerome Murphy-O'Connor, "The Second Letter to the Corinthians," in *The New Jerome Biblical Commentary*, ed. Raymond E. Brown, Joseph A. Fitzmyer, and Roland E. Murphy (Englewood Cliffs, NJ: Prentice Hall, 1990), 822.

chapter 4

Scriptural Evidence of Paul's Views on Women

This chapter reflects Paul's respect for the power of the feminine, particularly in the biblical personification of Sophia as well as the use of feminine imagery in his writings. Secondly, the chapter addresses Paul's writing about marriage as it reflects his belief in equality between men and women. The chapter then discusses Paul's citation of women in a variety of ministries and leadership roles, affirming his position for equality for women in leadership and service in the Church. Finally, the chapter considers certain "problem passages" that have traditionally led interpreters to conclude that Paul opposes women in ministry.

PAUL'S USE OF FEMININE IMAGERY

Woman Wisdom in the Old Testament and in Paul

The most striking personification in all of sacred Scripture is Woman Wisdom. The fundamental nature of the wisdom tradition includes both God's mighty deeds throughout human history and God's presence in everyday life with the give and take of its relationships. The wisdom tradition honors the holy mystery of people's lives as they live in the world: in the ordinary moments of each day, in the effort to be decent and just, in anguish over suffering and hardship, in reverence for all creation, in the struggle to harmoniously work out relationships, as well as in the peak experiences of personal and communal life.[1] Wisdom escapes the control of any one group, in

---

1. Elizabeth A. Johnson, "Redeeming the Name of Christ," in *Freeing Theology: The Essentials of Theology in Feminist Perspective*, ed. Catherine Mowry LaCugna (New York: HarperCollins, 1993), 122.

contrast to the traditions of cult and law, which were and, in many cases, continue to be preserved and maintained by the clergy.[2]

It is best to understand the feminine personification of Wisdom in her biblical expression as a communication of God.[3] In both the Old and New Testaments, *wisdom* is a feminine word, in Hebrew *hokmah* and in Greek *sophia*. In the biblical tradition of sapiential literature, Wisdom has divine origin (Proverbs 8:22; Sirach 24:3, 9; Wisdom 7:25–26). The key biblical passages in the sapiential literature that refer to Woman Wisdom are Job 28, Sirach 24, Baruch 3:9–4:4, Wisdom 7–9, and Proverbs 8.

The poetry in Job 28 proclaims that, although the earth abounds with a multitude of treasures that God has created, the most precious gift of all, wisdom, is beyond the grasp of humans. In fact, only the Creator God "knows the way to it" (Job 28:23). Distinct from the works of creation (for example, the abyss or the seas, Job 28:14), Wisdom is both present and visible to God.[4]

In the book of Sirach, Ben Sira writes that God alone knows the subtleties of wisdom: "It is he who created her; he saw her and took her measure; he poured her out upon all his works, upon all the living according to his gift; he lavished her upon those who love him" (Sirach 1:9–10, NRSV). wisdom was created before all things (Sirach 1:4) and those who fail to recognize her divine affiliation will not find her.[5] In Sirach 24, wisdom describes her origin: "From the mouth of the Most High I came forth" (24:3). She sings among the heavenly court in "the assembly of the Most High" (24:2). Similar to the spirit or breath of God that came over the waters of chaos (Genesis 1:1), wisdom describes herself as covering the earth in a "mistlike" manner (24:3).[6]

While the writings in the book of Job indicate that Woman Wisdom cannot be found, Baruch asserts that "she appeared on earth and lived with humankind" (3:37, NRSV). This verse cannot be

---

2. Roland E. Murphy, *The Tree of Life: An Exploration of Biblical Wisdom Literature* (Grand Rapids: Eerdmans, 2002), 133.

3. Ibid.

4. Ibid., 134.

5. Ibid., 133.

6. Ibid., 139.

eliminated as merely a Christian commentary.[7] The poetry in the book of Baruch identifies Woman Wisdom with the Torah: "She is the book of the commandments of God, the law that endures forever. All who hold her fast will live, and those who forsake her will die" (4:1, NRSV).

The Book of Wisdom portrays Wisdom as a spirit (*pneuma*); moreover, in Wisdom 9:17 she is parallel to "your holy spirit" sent from on high, and she is responsible for knowing the divine counsel. The twenty-one attributes of Woman Wisdom in 7:22–23 elaborate on her spiritual nature, indicating the kind of activity in which she engages. This incredible description of the personification of Wisdom superbly conveys the intimate relationship between God and Woman Wisdom: outpouring of divine glory, eternal light, mirror of divine activity, breath, and divine image.[8]

> For she is an aura of the might of God
> and a pure effusion of the glory of the Almighty;
> therefore nought that is sullied enters into her.
> For she is the refulgence of eternal light,
> the spotless mirror of the power of God,
> the image of his goodness. (Wisdom 7:25–26)

The most compelling and important text in the tradition of biblical wisdom literature regarding Woman Wisdom is Proverbs 8. Wisdom becomes a personal and active agent in the world, who is empowered by her own self-consciousness and will to act in order to effect life and well being (cf. Proverbs 1:20, 7:4, 8:1, 9:1).[9] In 8:12–16, Woman Wisdom describes the qualities that she confers, including prudence, counsel, knowledge, strength, understanding, and aversion to evil. The gift of understanding enables Woman Wisdom to be the basis for royal rule; these qualities are divine (Job 12:13), and they are gifts of the Lord's spirit to the messianic figure (Isaiah 11:2). Three times in Proverbs 8:32–34 there are commands

---

7. Ibid., 141.

8. Ibid., 143.

9. Walter Brueggemann, *Theology of the Old Testament: Testimony, Dispute, Advocacy* (Minneapolis: Augsburg Fortress Press, 1997), 343.

to listen to Wisdom, and blessings are directed to those who dedicate themselves to her pursuit.[10]

Two passages in the undisputed letters of Paul show awareness of the Wisdom tradition as expressed in Proverbs 8. In the first, Romans 11:33–36, Paul writes a doxology to the mysterious, hidden, and inscrutable intentionality of God, who will work out the divine purposes well beyond human reasoning and language.[11] In this hymn to wisdom, Paul's central assertion is that God's ways are beyond the grasp of human understanding. For Paul, the wisdom and the knowledge of God reverse and perplex human expectation, especially for those who hold dominant positions within any religious or political group. The wisdom of God includes all people in salvation. Through this hymn to wisdom, Paul seeks to appeal to all Christians with overwhelming sentiments of awe and praise designed to eradicate any doubts concerning the validity of his inclusive gospel.[12]

In the second passage, 1 Corinthians 1:18–25, Paul writes of Christ Jesus as "the wisdom of God" (v. 24) and refers to Christ Jesus as the one "who became for us wisdom from God" (v. 30). In these verses, Paul uses feminine imagery for Christ, alluding to the biblical tradition of Woman Wisdom. This illustrates Paul's paradoxical and revolutionary understanding of power and weakness as exemplified in Christ crucified, who is both the wisdom and the power of God, juxtaposed with human wisdom, which is foolishness, and human power, which is weakness. Paul speaks eloquently about the wisdom of God, which takes the form of foolishness and is made known in the Lord Jesus (v. 30).[13] Paul explains that he did not use Hellenistic rhetoric because this style of argument would have deprived the cross of Christ of its power.[14] Paul's summary description of the *kerygma* as "the message of the cross," literally "the word of the cross" (v. 18), is unique in the New Testament.[15] Paul presents human wisdom

---

10. Murphy, *Tree of Life*, 136.

11. Brueggemann, *Theology of the Old Testament*, 345.

12. Brendan Byrne, *Romans*, Sacra Pagina 6 (Collegeville, MN: Liturgical Press, 1996), 358.

13. Raymond Collins, *First Corinthians*, Sacra Pagina 7 (Collegeville, MN: Liturgical Press, 1999), 112.

14. Ibid., 101.

15. Ibid.

negatively in order to illustrate the point that human beings who consider themselves wise are, in fact, foolish. God's wisdom speaks judgment on the wisdom of human beings, which Paul says is "foolishness"; the wisdom of God will destroy this false notion of wisdom, rendering it invalid.[16]

In 1 Corinthians 10:4 Christ is personified as a "spiritual rock." Some scholars believe this also is a reference to the biblical figure of Divine Wisdom, since the rock[17] to which Paul alludes was identified with Woman Wisdom in some Jewish writings.[18]

In Philippians 3:7–11, Paul emphatically states that the "supreme good of knowing Christ Jesus my Lord" (v. 8) transcends and surpasses everything he has gained in life. The comparison of knowing Christ with "whatever gains I had" in Philippians 3:7–8 is similar to that of Woman Wisdom with all desirable goods depicted in Wisdom 7:7–10.[19] It is likely that the kenotic "hymn"[20] in Philippians 2:1–11 also has a wisdom background.[21]

Clearly, Paul had an understanding of and an appreciation for the sapiential tradition in which Woman Wisdom figures so prominently. Through her the community of faith is graced with the gifts and charisms needed for the growth and the unity of the nascent Church.

Other Examples of Feminine Imagery in Paul

Galatians 4:19

My children, for whom I am again in labor until Christ be formed in you!

Paul applied feminine imagery not only to Christ, but also in several instances to himself. In this passage Paul presents himself as a pregnant woman who struggles with the pangs of birth until the new life, Christ, is formed in those (the Galatians) whom he loves. This

---

16. Ibid., 92.

17. Exodus 17:6; Numbers 20:7–11.

18. Veronica Koperski, *The Knowledge of Christ Jesus My Lord: The High Christology of Philippians 3:7–11* (Kampen, The Netherlands: Kok Pharos, 1996), 306.

19. Ibid., 299.

20. Some scholars, e.g., Gordon Fee, do not regard this text as a hymn.

21. Koperski, *The Knowledge of Christ Jesus my Lord*, 298–99.

imagery is complex[22] but also familiar. The realization that Christ is not yet "formed" in the Galatians propels Paul into pain that he identifies with the intensity of labor pains, until Christ is formed in the community of believers. Christ takes form in the life and ministry of the Galatian churches as believers conform themselves to the crucified one.[23] The birth metaphor is also used in Romans 8:22. This passage widens the context to that of God's reign: the "whole creation has been groaning in labor pains" in anticipation of the redemption. In Galatians 4:19, as Christ is being formed in the community of faith, it is Paul who experiences the labor pains.[24]

1 Thessalonians 2:7

[. . .] although we were able to impose our weight as apostles of Christ. Rather, we were gentle among you, as a nursing mother cares for her children.

The feminine imagery in this passage is tender and nurturing, indicating the intensity of human love. Paul uses this maternal imagery to remind the Thessalonians of the depth of his concern and affection for them, sharing not only the gospel but also his very self (1 Thessalonians 2:8), as a mother nourishes her child with milk from her breast.[25] Paul indicates that the apostles related to the community at Thessalonica with love and compassion rather than with the authority and power that were rightfully theirs as apostles. This attitude illustrates Paul's understanding that apostleship is not for domination, but rather for nurturing. With this metaphor of intimate relationship Paul redefines the role of Church authority as self-giving servant leadership rather than focusing on the inherent power of ecclesiastical structures. He addresses the Thessalonians tenderly and with great affection.[26]

---

22. Frank Matera, *Galatians*, Sacra Pagina 9 (Collegeville, MN: Liturgical Press, 1992), 166.

23. Ibid., 167.

24. Kristen Plinke Bentley and Sharyn Dowd, "Galatians," in *The IVP Women's Bible Commentary*, ed. Catherine Clark Kroeger and Mary J. Evans (Downers Grove, IL: InterVarsity, 2002), 686.

25. Margo G. Houts, "Paul's Use of Female Imagery," in *The IVP Women's Bible Commentary*, ed. Catherine Clark Kroeger and Mary J. Evans (Downers Grove, IL: InterVarsity, 2002), 725.

26. Ibid., 725–26.

1 Corinthians 3:2

I fed you milk, not solid food, because you were unable to take it. Indeed, you are still not able, even now.

Paul reprimands the Corinthian community for their spiritual immaturity. They are not yet ready to be weaned from milk and given solid food (1 Corinthians 3:2).[27] Since the Corinthians were not capable of spiritually sustaining themselves when Paul was not present with them, or at the time of his writing, he confronts and admonishes them about their need and the importance of his role in their nurturing.[28] The issue of capability is a critical component of Paul's exhortations to the Christian community of faith in Corinth.

The early Church was conscious of and responsive to female images and feminine symbols of ministry. Augustine wrote, "Like Christ, apostolic ministry resembled both fatherhood and motherhood."[29] A third-century fresco in the Priscilla catacombs in Rome depicts three distinct, yet related, images of women engaged in ministry: a woman in prayer with arms raised, a woman suckling an infant, and a bishop who appears to be ordaining a woman. Some scholars suggest that this may have been based on Paul's imagery of a mother nursing her child to memorialize the intimate, nurturing, and self-giving example and words of Paul as he boldly challenged the ministers in the Christian communities.[30]

Galatians 4:21–31

Tell me, you who want to be under the law, do you not listen to the law? For it is written that Abraham had two sons, one by the slave woman and the other by the freeborn woman. The son of the slave woman was born naturally, the son of the freeborn through a promise. Now this is an allegory. These women represent two covenants. One was from Mount Sinai, bearing children for slavery; this is

---

27. Ibid., 726.

28. Collins, *First Corinthians*, 143.

29. *Enarratio in Psalmum* (*Enarrations on the Psalms*) 101, PL 37, col. 1299, cited in Houts, "Paul's Use of Female Imagery," 726.

30. Houts, "Paul's Use of Female Imagery," 726.

Hagar. Hagar represents Sinai, a mountain in Arabia; it corresponds to the present Jerusalem, for she is in slavery along with her children. But the Jerusalem above is freeborn, and she is our mother. For it is written:

> "Rejoice, you barren one who bore no children;
> break forth and shout, you who were not in labor;
> for more numerous are the children of the deserted
> one than of her who has a husband."

Now you, brothers, like Isaac, are children of the promise. But just as then the child of the flesh persecuted the child of the spirit, it is the same now. But what does the scripture say?

"Drive out the slave woman and her son! For the son of the slave woman shall not share the inheritance with the son" of the freeborn. Therefore, brothers, we are children not of the slave woman but of the freeborn woman.

Although some have found problems in this passage,[31] Paul is neither encouraging the mistreatment of slaves, nor being pejorative about the laws of the Mosaic covenant, nor making a negative judgment about women. Here Paul uses the allegory of slavery for rhetorical purposes to compare the freedom of God's covenant promise and faith in Christ to the slavery of the law of the Mosaic covenant. The use of Sarah to represent the covenant of freedom indicates that, in order to be a child of this covenant, it is insufficient only to claim Abraham as father. The promise is conveyed through both mother and father.

EQUALITY IN MARRIAGE

In the following passages, Paul gives equivalent advice to both husbands and wives. In 1 Corinthians 7:2–5, Paul's advice to married people is given in a parallel structure: he outlines the responsibilities and the duties that a husband fulfills for his wife and, likewise, what a wife is to do for her husband. Paul's attitude of parity in sex and marriage in 7:1–16 is meant to apply equally to both men and

---

31. See Plinke Bentley and Dowd, "Galatians," 686–87, regarding problematic aspects of Galatians 4:21–31.

women.[32] He calls for unity expressed in the mutuality of sexual intimacy in marriage. Paul does not assert that the physical body of the wife belongs to the husband, or equally, that the physical body of the husband belongs to the wife. He refers to the whole person, emphasizing that neither the wife nor the husband enjoys complete autonomy but rather the two belong mutually to one another.[33] In this letter, Paul expresses his understanding of the authority and responsibilities of both women and men in the marriage relationship. His words transcend the common understanding in the Hellenistic world, which emphasized the rights of men over women, particularly in marriage where the woman was considered property. Paul's challenge to mutual respect and parity in sexual intimacy engendered a sense of hope in women and in others who were alienated and who lived on the fringes of society. By gracing people with hope, Paul made Christianity attractive to oppressed peoples including slaves, women, and those who had no status in the religious or cultural spheres.

In 1 Corinthians 7:10–16, Paul equally advises a wife not to separate from her husband and a husband not to divorce his wife (see related discussion in chapter 3). In this section, Paul first addresses the situation of a wife divorcing her husband in a way that is distinct from how his other exhortations employ the oral tradition of Jesus' words. It appears that Paul was aware of a situation in Corinth where a wife had divorced, or was about to divorce, her husband.[34] In verse 15, Paul makes an exception when a spouse who is not a Christian is unwilling to remain married to the Christian partner. In such cases, Paul directs that the non-Christian partner be allowed to separate.[35]

EQUALITY IN MINISTRY

Paul is adamant that the spiritual gifts and charisms, though given to the individual, are for the benefit of the community of faith. They are not for personal enhancement, but are bestowed upon each person for the common good of all believers (1 Corinthians 12:7). Each

---

32. Collins, *First Corinthians*, 258.

33. Ibid., 259.

34. Ibid., 269.

35. Ibid., 271.

person serves the Lord Jesus Christ and the Christian community through gifts given by the Spirit. Paul's criteria for evaluating gifts and charisms are first that the gifts are not for the individual but are to be placed at the disposal of the community of faith for the common good, and second that each individual receives the gifts from the Spirit as the Spirit wills.[36] Paul vehemently contests anyone's claim to exclusive possession of the Spirit and the gifts of the Spirit. Paul's language emphasizes the utterly gratuitous love and copious generosity of the Spirit, who bestows the gifts and the charisms upon individuals for the benefit of the entire community of faith.[37]

In 1 Corinthians 12:11, Paul insists that the purpose of the gifts in the community is to promote unity and that those in the community should revere the variety of gifts. He stresses the importance of interrelationships within the community, and he discourages dominance and arrogance because they destroy relationships and, consequently, unity.

Paul states that God, working through the presence of the Holy Spirit, is the source of all of the gifts given to the community of faith. Anyone who disdains the gifts given to any member disdains the work of the Spirit. The Spirit is given to any member of the faith community as the Spirit wills, not as individuals with power in religious systems or institutions may choose. Paul argues that the one who does not honor the call and the gifts of each individual in the community disregards the Spirit of God, who graces the community with the variety of gifts for the good of the Church. Respecting the gifts given to any member honors the Holy Spirit, who is the source of every good gift. To the extent that people choose to deny the gifts and the call of individuals within the Church based on human, systemic, and institutional practices and "laws," they deny the activity of the Holy Spirit within the Church. God acts within the community of faith through the gifts of the Spirit present in each Christian.[38] Honoring the gifts given to each person is, in essence, honoring the Holy Spirit.

Paul teaches that no one can claim exclusive possession of the Spirit of God.[39] He reminds the community that each person, male

---

36. Ibid., 450.
37. Ibid.
38. Ibid.
39. Ibid., 451.

and female, has one or more of the gifts, but no one person, class, or gender has all of the gifts. In this community of faith where each individual has become a new creation in Christ, the social, economic, and gender divisions have been eradicated by virtue of baptism into the one Spirit.[40]

WOMEN MINISTERS IN PAUL

The plethora of citations in the undisputed letters of Paul makes it abundantly clear that Paul holds the ministry of women in high esteem. The terms that he uses to describe women's leadership positions and their ministries in the early Church are the same terms he applies to men and to himself and his ministry. These terms include "apostle," "deacon" (not "deaconess"), "co-worker," "countryman," "yokemate," and "hard workers."[41] Undoubtedly, the presence of Paul's commendations of women in his writings were as striking in the first century as they are in the twenty-first and would have been difficult to dismiss before Church tradition found ways to ignore and sadly even to eradicate them. In truth, the role of women in the Pauline communities was much greater and more nearly equal to that of men than one finds in contemporary Christianity.

Apphia

[. . .] to Apphia our sister, to Archippus our fellow soldier, and to the church at your house. (Philemon 2)

The exact position held by Apphia in the house church addressed in the Letter to Philemon is uncertain. Traditionally Apphia is accepted as the wife of Philemon. Perhaps Paul named Apphia in this letter based on his understanding of the cultural context of the *paterfamilias*. Specifically, Apphia, as a wife, would have been responsible for managing the household, which included supervision of the slaves, one of whom, Onesimus, is the subject of Paul's Letter to Philemon. Some scholars suggest that perhaps Paul's purpose in naming Apphia

---

40. Elisabeth Schüssler Fiorenza, "1 Corinthians," in *The HarperCollins Bible Commentary*, ed. James L. Mays (New York: HarperCollins, 1988), 1088.

41. Bonnie Bowman Thurston, "Paul's Greetings to Female Colleagues," in *The IVP Women's Bible Commentary*, ed. Catherine Clark Kroeger and Mary J. Evans (Downers Grove, IL: InterVarsity, 2002), 712.

and designating her as "sister" in this letter may have been to insure that she, a woman patron of equal or greater means than Philemon, knew of Paul's instructions regarding Onesimus and might appeal to Philemon on Paul's behalf.[42]

Chloe

> For it has been reported to me about you, my brothers, by Chloe's people, that there are rivalries among you. (1 Corinthians 1:11)

Since *koinonia*[43] is the foundation of Christian life and its only authentic expression, Paul's primary concern in this passage is lack of unity among the Christians at Corinth.[44] Regrettably, we know little or nothing about Chloe, save that Paul felt that she was well acquainted with the Corinthian situation and that her alarming report of conditions there was thoroughly reliable.[45] Since Paul recognizes those who came to him with her concerns, it is likely that Chloe was a leader in the Christian community in Corinth and probably the head of a church that gathered in her home (cf. Acts 16:15; Romans 16:10; Colossians 4:15).[46] Paul responds to the serious concerns that the messengers presented in Chloe's name, addressing the rivalries that threatened the new community of faith at Corinth.

Euodia and Syntyche

> I urge Euodia and I urge Syntyche to come to a mutual understanding in the Lord. Yes, and I ask you also, my true yokemate, to help them, for they have struggled at

---

42. Pheme Perkins, "Philemon," in *The Women's Bible Commentary*, ed. Carol A. Newsom and Sharon H. Ringe (Louisville, KY: Westminster John Knox Press, 1998), 453.

43. The Greek word connoting the fellowship, sharing, and breaking of the bread within the early Church.

44. Jerome Murphy-O'Connor, "The First Letter to the Corinthians," in *The New Jerome Biblical Commentary*, ed. Raymond E. Brown, Joseph A. Fitzmyer, and Roland E. Murphy (Englewood Cliffs, NJ: Prentice Hall, 1990), 800.

45. Mary Ann Getty, "1 Corinthians," in *The Collegeville Bible Commentary*, ed. Robert J. Karris (Collegeville, MN: Liturgical Press, 1992), 1107.

46. Collins, *First Corinthians*, 78.

my side in promoting the gospel, along with Clement and
my other co-workers, whose names are in the book of life.
(Philippians 4:2–3)

In the Christian community at Philippi, we encounter women
leaders, Euodia and Syntyche, who apparently minister without
male counterparts. Some scholars suggest that the "yokemate"
referred to in verse 3 is perhaps Lydia, a dealer of purple cloth
(Acts 16:14); however, this is conjecture.[47] Nevertheless, most
scholars would agree that women served in positions of leadership
in the community at Philippi.[48] Additionally, it is important to
recognize that the manner in which Paul describes these women as
participating with him in the work of the gospel implies that they
were involved in the evangelization of nonbelievers.[49] In a homily
addressing Paul's Letter to the Philippians, Saint John Chrysostom (c. 347–407), bishop of Constantinople, Father and doctor of
the Church, remarks, "It appears to me that these women were the
heads of the church at Philippi."[50]

Conspicuous by its absence in Philippians is any reference by
Paul to his authority as apostle, father, or mother to the community.
He bases his exhortation on their mutual affection in Christ.[51] Paul
affirms that Euodia and Syntyche have worked with him on an equal
basis, explicitly stating that these women have "struggled" at his side.
He exhorts Euodia and Syntyche to reconcile their disagreement
in order to enhance their leadership and to facilitate greater unity
within the community of faith at Philippi. In fact, Paul considers
the authority of Euodia and Syntyche in the community at Philippi

47. Ronald F. Hock, "Philippians," in *The HarperCollins Bible Commentary*, ed. James
L. Mays (New York: HarperCollins, 1988), 1124.

48. Karen Jo Torjesen, *When Women Were Priests: Women's Leadership in the Early
Church and the Scandal of their Subordination in the Rise of Christianity* (San Francisco:
HarperCollins, 1993), 16.

49. Margaret Y. MacDonald, "Reading Real Women Through the Undisputed Letters
of Paul," in *Women and Christian Origins*, ed. Ross Shepard Kraemer and Mary Rose
D'Angelo (New York: Oxford University Press, 1999), 205.

50. Homily 13, cited in Veronica Koperski, "Philippians," in *The IVP Women's Bible
Commentary*, ed. Catherine Clark Kroeger and Mary J. Evans (Downers Grove, IL:
InterVarsity, 2002), 706.

51. Ibid., 709.

so great that their dissention seriously damaged the Christian mission.[52] In Philippians 4:2 Paul admonishes Euodia and Syntyche "to be of the same mind" (NRSV) and reminds them that at stake in this disagreement is not merely a personal quarrel, but, more importantly, the shared commitment and purpose of their equal partnership in the "race" for the gospel.[53]

Prisca

> Greet Prisca and Aquila, my co-workers in Christ Jesus, who risked their necks for my life, to whom not only I am grateful but also all the churches of the Gentiles; greet also the church at their house. (Romans 16:3–5a; cf. Acts 18:1–26; 1 Corinthians 16:19)

Prisca and Aquila were eminent missionary co-workers of Paul who did not stand under his authority, as did Barnabas and Apollos.[54] They are mentioned six times in the New Testament (Acts 18:2–3, 18–19, 26; Romans 16:3; 1 Corinthians 16:19; 2 Timothy 4:19). The author of Luke/Acts refers to Prisca with the familial derivation or nickname, Priscilla, which is translated, "Little Prisca."[55]

Following the edict of Claudius (49 CE), Jews and Jewish Christians were expelled from Rome due to civic unrest. Leaving Rome, Prisca and Aquila went to Corinth where they established their residence and their trade and were able to provide Paul with a base of operations, a place to live, and a shop where he carried on the mission of evangelization for eighteen months (Acts 18:11).[56] Acts 18:1–3 describes Paul's introduction to Prisca and Aquila, a married couple who were living the way of the Lord. They practiced the same trade as Paul (Act 18:3) and their home was the house church in Corinth where the community of faith met. Upon leaving Corinth

---

52. Elizabeth Schüssler Fiorenza, *In Memory of Her: A Feminist Theological Reconstruction of Christian Origins* (New York: Crossroad, 1989), 170.

53. Ibid., 170.

54. Elisabeth Schüssler Fiorenza, *But She Said: Feminist Practices of Biblical Interpretation* (Boston: Beacon Press, 1992), 168.

55. Mary Ann Getty-Sullivan, *Women in the New Testament* (Collegeville, MN: Liturgical Press, 2001), 155.

56. Collins, *First Corinthians*, 608.

with Paul, they sailed to Syria, traveled to Cenchreae, and finally reached Ephesus (Acts 18:18–19).

In Ephesus, Prisca and Aquila once again opened their home to the Christian community as a house church. It was from Ephesus that Paul wrote the greeting to the Christian community in Corinth (1 Corinthians 16:19), sharing with them greetings in the Lord from Prisca and Aquila and the church that met at their house. From these greetings (Romans 16:3–5 and 1 Corinthians 16:19) along with Acts 18:1–21, we can ascertain that the home of Prisca and Aquila was, in fact, a house church for the Christian communities in Corinth, in Ephesus, and in Rome.[57]

Since Priscilla (Prisca) is named first in Acts 18:26, some scholars posit that she was the chief teacher who instructed the renowned Apollos[58] in the faith. The author of Luke/Acts describes Apollos as from Alexandria, educated there, and "well-versed in the scriptures" (Acts 18:24, NRSV). Probably Prisca, too, was very well educated.

In four of six New Testament references (Acts 18:18, 26; Romans 16:3; 2 Timothy 4:19) Prisca's name appears before that of her husband, Aquila. This may be due to her greater social status, but more likely reflects her greater prominence within the Christian community.[59] Additionally, many scholars feel that perhaps Paul, and later Luke, intended to emphasize the essential roles of women in the mission of early Christianity.[60]

In describing Prisca and Aquila in the Letter to the Romans, Paul names them "co-workers," his partners, and his equals in ministry and in Christ. He relates to the community the dangers that they courageously suffered while risking their lives for him and, ultimately, for the Lord Jesus Christ. In referring to Prisca and Aquila as "co-workers," Paul clearly indicates that Prisca and Aquila share in the same work of ministry in which he is involved (cf. Romans 16:9, 21; 1 Corinthians 16:16; Philemon 1).[61] Paul reminds the Christian community in Rome that not only are they indebted to

---

57. Getty-Sullivan, *Women in the New Testament*, 157.

58. Acts 18:24; 19:1; 1 Corinthians 1:12; 3:4, 5, 6, 22; 4:6; 16:12.

59. Getty-Sullivan, *Women in the New Testament*, 154.

60. Collins, *First Corinthians*, 609.

61. Craig S. Keener, *Paul, Women and Wives: Marriage and Women's Ministry in the Letters of Paul* (Peabody, MA: Hendrickson, 1992), 241.

Prisca and Aquila, but so too are all of the Christian communities of the Gentiles.

Phoebe

I commend to you Phoebe our sister, who is (also) a minister of the church at Cenchreae, that you may receive her in the Lord in a manner worthy of the holy ones, and help her in whatever she may need from you, for she has been a benefactor to many and to me as well. (Romans 16:1–2)

As the probable bearer[62] of the Letter to the Romans, Phoebe is commended to the community of faith. By citing Phoebe's Church offices as "sister," "deacon" (*diakonos*), and "benefactor" or "sponsor" (*prostatis*), Paul implies that she has the authority to explain his letter to the Christian community in Rome.[63]

In spite of the inherent authority and high esteem with which Paul commends Phoebe, tragically, her significance for the early Church, as well as for the Church today, has been diminished due to grammatically altered translations that change the meaning of Paul's words. The Greek word *diakonos*, although grammatically masculine, in relationship to Phoebe traditionally is translated "deaconess." By substituting this word, Phoebe's diaconal role is reduced to that of the subservient and female-oriented task of the deaconess in later Christian history.[64] However, when Paul uses the word *diakonos* in other contexts, he refers to individuals who preach and teach as official congregational leaders in the early Christian communities.[65] Furthermore, the Greek *prostasis* is usually translated in reference to Phoebe as "helper" or "patroness"; however, in the first century the word commonly meant a leader, president, or superintendent.[66]

Even though Phoebe (Romans 16:1–2) is unique in that no one else in the writings of Paul is given three significant titles (sister,

---

62. Brendan Byrne, states that Phoebe is "almost certainly the bearer of his letter to Rome." Byrne, *Romans*, 447.

63. Keener, *Paul, Women and Wives*, 238.

64. Barbara J. MacHaffie, *Her Story: Women in Christian Tradition* (Philadelphia: Fortress Press, 1986), 25.

65. Ibid.

66. Ibid.

deacon [*diakonos*], and benefactor [*prostatis*]) and receives a letter of recommendation from Paul, her importance is overlooked time and again. Biblical exegetes tend to minimize these titles or to interpret them differently when referring to Phoebe, in contrast to when the titles refer to men. The only exception to the translation of the word *diakonos* as "minister," "missionary," or "servant" is when it is translated as "deaconess" in reference to Phoebe. Paul does not name her a deaconess, ministering exclusively to women; he names her a deacon (*diakonos*), implying that she is in fact a minister to the entire Christian Church.[67]

Understanding the meaning of the Greek words *diakonos* and *prostasis*, then, one can plausibly assume that Phoebe not only held great authority in the community of faith in Cenchreae, but that she also was held in great esteem throughout the early Christian communities.

The noteworthy role of Phoebe in the early Church, and by extension the value of her role for the Church today, is that she exemplifies the leadership roles exercised by women in the early Church. The Letter to the Romans has been held in esteem throughout Christian history as one of the most influential writings of the New Testament. In light of this, it is momentous that Paul entrusted this woman, Phoebe, to deliver this letter. He recognized the grueling journey that she would have to make and understood that the acceptance of the message was dependent upon the respect afforded to the messenger.[68]

Mary

Greet Mary, who has worked hard for you. (Romans 16:6)

Mary is greeted and named because of her arduous work for the Christian community. In describing her ministry, Paul uses the verb "worked" or "labored" (*kopian*). Since this verb describes Paul's apostolic ministry to proclaim the good news (1 Corinthians 15:10; Galatians 4:11; Philippians 2:16), this is substantial testimony to the apostolic activity of women in the early Church.[69] Other examples

---

67. Schüssler Fiorenza, *In Memory of Her*, 170.

68. Byrne, *Romans*, 448.

69. Ibid., 451.

of Paul using the verb "worked" (*kopian*) as indications of laboring for the gospel are to be found in 1 Corinthians 16:16 and 1 Thessalonians 5:12. In Romans 16 Paul consistently applies this verb to women: Mary (v. 6), Tryphaena, Tryphosa, and Persis (v. 12).[70]

Junia

Greet Andronicus and Junia, my relatives and my fellow prisoners; they are prominent among the apostles and they were in Christ before me. (Romans 16:7)

Junia is a feminine Latin name that is here transliterated into Greek as *Iounia*.[71] Because this name is grammatically the object of the verb "greet," it occurs in the accusative case in this verse: *Iounian*. This is an ambiguous form. It could either be the accusative of *Iounia* (a feminine name) or *Iounias* (which would be masculine). The problem is, while *Iounia* is a fairly common girl's name in antiquity, there is no evidence whatsoever for any man with the name *Iounias*. The name *Iounias* is grammatically possible, but to the best of our knowledge it did not exist in Paul's day. During the late Medieval and Reformation periods (1500s), especially under the influence of Martin Luther's translation,[72] it was regularly assumed that the individual Paul greets in Romans 16:7 must be male, because Paul calls this person an "apostle." In effect, rather than admit that Paul called a woman an apostle, later interpreters posited the existence of a "boy named Sue." There is no evidence in inscriptions, public monuments, graffiti, literature, or any other ancient source that the masculine form of this name existed in the first century CE. It is the creation of later Church leaders, uncomfortable with the scriptural evidence of a woman apostle who had leadership within the Church.[73]

---

70. Lynn H. Cohick, "Romans," in *The IVP Women's Bible Commentary*, ed. Catherine Clark Kroeger and Mary J. Evans (Downers Grove, IL: InterVarsity, 2002), 644.

71. Ibid.

72. Luise Schottroff, *Let the Oppressed Go Free: Feminist Perspectives on the New Testament*, trans. Annemarie S. Kidder (Louisville, KY: Westminster/John Knox Press, 1991), 36.

73. Cohick, "Romans," 645.

The earlier Church leaders, however, knew better. John Chrysostom, a Church Father of the fourth century, had no doubt that Paul was addressing a woman, Junia, in Romans 16:7. He states: "'Indeed to be apostles at all is a great thing. . . . But to be even amongst these of note, just consider what an encomium this is! . . . Oh how great is the devotion of this woman, that she should be counted worthy of the appellation of apostle!'" (NPNF 1st series, 11:555).[74]

Paul informs the Christian community that Junia was "in Christ" before him and that her active ministry has brought her, like himself, into captivity. By recalling Junia's imprisonment, Paul places her *expressis verbis* in the tradition of the apostolic discipleship of the cross.[75]

Tryphaena and Tryphosa, and Persis

Greet those workers in the Lord, Tryphaena and Tryphosa.
Greet the beloved Persis, who has worked hard in the Lord.
(Romans 16:12)

Although we know very little about Tryphaena and Tryphosa, the fact that Paul greets them as "workers in the Lord" indicates that they were women in missionary ministry. Tryphaena and Tryphosa were involved in a missionary partnership; most likely they were sisters, possibly twins.[76] Paul may have consciously drawn out the ironical contrast between their names, connected with the Greek word for "softness" (*tryphe*), and their having "worked hard" for the Lord Jesus Christ.[77]

In greeting Persis and in describing her ministry in the Christian community, Paul uses the same verb, "worked" or "labored" (*kopian*), with which he describes his own apostolic ministry (1 Corinthians 15:10; Galatians 4:11; Philippians 2:16).[78]

---

74. Chrysostom does not seem to have any difficulty with the idea of a woman apostle, even as he has no difficulty with considering Euodia and Syntyche heads of the church at Philippi.

75. Ute E. Eisen, *Women Officeholders in Early Christianity: Epigraphical and Literary Studies*, trans. Linda M. Maloney, (Collegeville, MN: Liturgical Press, 2000), 49.

76. Byrne, *Romans*, 454.

77. Ibid.

78. Ibid., 451.

The Mother of Rufus

Greet Rufus, chosen in the Lord, and his mother and mine. (Romans 16:13)

While the name of the mother of Rufus is not mentioned in this greeting, her ministry of hospitality, maternal kindness, and concern for Paul is noteworthy. Paul's esteem for this unnamed woman is implicit as he greets her, declaring that he considers her as his own mother. Throughout the ages, God has blessed women who engage in the ministry of mothering those who are not of their own blood.[79]

Julia, Olympas, and the Sister of Nereus

Greet Philologus, Julia, Nereus and his sister, and Olympas, and all the holy ones who are with them. (Romans 16:15)

All of those greeted in this passage are probably involved in missionary work. We can infer that the inclusion of the sister of Nereus indicates that the unnamed woman and her brother are engaged in ministry as missionary partners. The foundation for this assertion is in the use of the Greek word *adelphe*, "sister," which indicates an official title in her significance for the Christian community since she is not mentioned as a "wife."[80]

The plethora of citations in the undisputed letters of Paul clearly demonstrates that Paul holds the ministry of women in high esteem. He uses terms that describe women's leadership positions and their ministries in the early Church that are equal to the terms he applies to men and identical to the terms he uses to describe himself and his ministry.

Does Paul Make Negative References to Women?

The passages discussed above demonstrate Paul's appreciation for many women who were active in ministry in Paul's day. Yet, in many quarters Paul continues to be accused of misogyny. It is time to consider several passages that are often cited as evidence that Paul held a negative view of women and opposed women in ministry.

---

79. Cohick, "Romans," 645.

80. Schüssler Fiorenza, *In Memory of Her*, 180.

REGARDING WOMEN'S VEILS
(1 CORINTHIANS 11:2-16)

(2) I praise you because you remember me in everything and hold fast to the traditions, just as I handed them on to you. (3) But I want you to know that Christ is the head of every man, and a husband the head of his wife, and God the head of Christ. (4) Any man who prays or prophesies with his head covered brings shame upon his head. (5) But any woman who prays or prophesies with her head unveiled brings shame upon her head, for it is one and the same thing as if she had had her head shaved. (6) For if a woman does not have her head veiled, she may as well have her hair cut off. But if it is shameful for a woman to have her hair cut off or her head shaved, then she should wear a veil.

(7) A man, on the other hand, should not cover his head, because he is the image and glory of God, but woman is the glory of man. (8) For man did not come from woman, but woman from man; (9) nor was man created for woman, but woman for man; (10) for this reason a woman should have a sign of authority on her head, because of the angels. (11) Woman is not independent of man or man of woman in the Lord. (12) For just as woman came from man, so man is born of woman; but all things are from God.

(13) Judge for yourselves: is it proper for a woman to pray to God with her head unveiled? (14) Does not nature itself teach you that if a man wears his hair long it is a disgrace to him, (15) whereas if a woman has long hair it is her glory, because long hair has been given (her) for a covering? (16) But if anyone is inclined to be argumentative, we do not have such a custom, nor do the churches of God.

An initial reading of this text might suggest that Paul claims women are inferior and subordinate to men. Indeed the material in verses 2–9 seems to imply this attitude; however, concluding his scriptural argument in verses 11–12, Paul offers a corrective. While the issue being addressed at the beginning of the passage may have been gender-specific, Paul's ultimate view of creation and the new order in the Lord is both comprehensive and egalitarian. Paul's instruction in verse 11 reminds the Christian believer that ultimately men and women share a common nature; there is no difference in that woman is from man and men are born from women. Paul's commentary in verse 12 explains that from the Christian perspective of creation there is a fundamental parity between men and women.[81]

The context of Paul's injunctions concerning the behavior of women during worship services in the Christian community demonstrates that women, as well as men, share in the gifts of the Spirit, and prophesy and pray publicly under the influence of the divine Spirit.[82] Paul begins this section by affirming the behavior of the community for following his teaching and his example (11:2), and he neither prohibits nor discourages this "spiritual" self-understanding and practice of the Corinthians.[83]

In first-century Corinth, the ways in which men and women wore their hair indicated their social, financial, and religious status. Paul was concerned with proper hairstyles and proper attire for both men and women. As Paul addressed other issues dealing with the behavior of a few problematic women that threatened the community, the principle of mutuality, so frequently evident in the writings of Paul, dominates his discussion. However, it appears that the real issue here is proper attire and proper hairstyles as an indication of appropriate order.[84] Paul's concern to avoid "shame" (v. 5) in particular suggests that the heart of the issue here was that women, when participating in worship, ought not to dress in a way that their culture considers inappropriate. In fact, this passage demonstrates that Paul knows of and accepts the participation of women, praying and prophesying, in *public* worship services (provided that they dress appropriately), for "shame" results from immodest dress only when worn in public, not in the privacy of one's own home. Paul's aim is not to reaffirm gender differences, but to insist on decency and right order for all involved in worship. Paul assures the community of faith in Corinth that he does not want to hinder prophetic speaking or

---

81. Collins, *First Corinthians*, 402–3.

82. Schüssler Fiorenza, *In Memory of Her*, 226.

83. Ibid.

84. Collins, *First Corinthians*, 396.

speaking in tongues, but rather is concerned that everything "must be done properly and in order" (1 Corinthians 14:40).[85]

The point of the entire passage is Paul's praise for the Christian community at Corinth for holding on to the traditions he has transmitted to them, women and men alike. These traditions meant liberation, freedom, equality, and Spirit-empowerment in Christ and in the Lord.[86] In verse 10, using the Greek *exousian*, "authority," which clearly means authority to be exercised, Paul takes for granted the leadership role that women play in the Christian community in Corinth.[87]

WOMEN KEEPING SILENT IN THE CHURCHES (1 CORINTHIANS 14:33B–36)

> (33b) As in all the churches of the holy ones, (34) women should keep silent in the churches, for they are not allowed to speak, but should be subordinate, as even the law says. (35) But if they want to learn anything, they should ask their husbands at home. For it is improper for a woman to speak in the church. (36) Did the word of God go forth from you? Or has it come to you alone?

Many will argue that the literal interpretation of this passage throughout the centuries has thwarted the exercise of the Holy Spirit's gifts to women for the benefit of the Christian community of faith. For anyone who values equality, particularly for women, the exhortation that women be silent is distressing and problematic from the perspective of first-century Corinth—to say nothing of the second and third millennia. This pericope expresses a viewpoint that obviously contradicts Paul's previous statements regarding the prominent role of women in worship (1 Corinthians 11:5, 13). Why would he assume, as he does in chapter 11, that women may pray and prophesy in the assembled church if they are appropriately attired, only to turn around in chapter 14 and insist that they not even speak

---

85. Schüssler Fiorenza, *In Memory of Her*, 226.

86. Ibid., 228.

87. Murphy-O'Connor, "The First Letter to the Corinthians," 809.

in church? Additionally, Paul's invocation of the Law to support the submission of women contradicts not only what he says elsewhere on the subject of women (e.g., Galatians 3:28), but also on the role of the Law for Christians in general (Romans 10:4; Galatians 4:9).[88]

A common claim supported by textual criticism[89] asserts that this passage likely originated as a marginal note by a deutropauline scribe rather than Paul himself; as such, it was a later addition to the text. The appeal to the Law (possibly Genesis 3:16) is not only un-Pauline, but contradicts 1 Corinthians 11:5. The injunctions against women reflect the misogyny of 1 Timothy 2:11–14, discussed below, which most likely originated from the same deutropauline scribes.[90]

Paul exhorts the Christian community at Corinth to remember that the Spirit decides who will receive the gift of prophecy (12:11). From 1 Corinthians 11:5, it is clear that Paul believes that some of those to whom the Spirit has given the gift of prophecy are women. The entire community benefits from the gift of prophecy given by the Spirit to both men and women (14:1–5). To prohibit the gift of the Spirit by impeding a woman so endowed from speaking within the assembly is to place a restriction on God's working within the community of faith.[91]

---

88. Getty, "1 Corinthians," 1128.

89. Specifically, the passage in question does not occur in the same place in all manuscripts; while most insert it after v. 33a, a number of important early manuscripts place it after v. 40—where it interrupts the flow of Paul's thought just as badly as it does here. Textual critics have found that passages like this, which have no fixed place in the text and seem not to fit in any of the locations they are found, are often later additions to the text. Some scribe writes a note in the margin, perhaps for his own reference, and much later copyists come upon it, assume it is part of the original text, and attempt to work it into their copy of the text wherever it seems to fit best, some in one part of the manuscript, some in another. A classic example of this phenomenon is the passage about the woman taken in adultery, which is found in John 7:53–8:11 in printed editions of the Bible, but which actually occurs in a number of places in the original manuscripts; most scholars conclude that it is not original to the text.

90. Murphy-O'Connor, "The First Letter to the Corinthians," 811.

91. Ibid.

A RED HERRING (1 TIMOTHY 2:8–15)

It is my wish, then, that in every place the men should pray, lifting up holy hands, without anger or argument. Similarly, (too,) women should adorn themselves with proper conduct, with modesty and self-control, not with braided hairstyles and gold ornaments, or pearls, or expensive clothes, but rather, as befits women who profess reverence for God, with good deeds. A woman must receive instruction silently and under complete control. I do not permit a woman to teach or to have authority over a man. She must be quiet. For Adam was formed first, then Eve. Further, Adam was not deceived, but the woman was deceived and transgressed. But she will be saved through motherhood, provided women persevere in faith and love and holiness, with self-control.

It is difficult to see in this passage anything other than a denial that women may exercise any teaching or authoritative role in the Church. As such, 1 Timothy 2:8–15 is often taken as evidence of Paul's conservative attitude toward women in ministry. This, however, is a mistake, for there is almost universal agreement among biblical scholars that First Timothy is Deutro-Pauline. That is to say, Paul did not write this. Rather, it comes from a group of followers of Paul who attempted to carry on his legacy in the generation after his death by continuing to produce documents in Paul's name, attempting to bring Paul's theology to bear on the problems of the Church in their day. In this instance it would seem that they did a poor job of representing Paul's thought. First Timothy 2:8–15 can contribute nothing to our understanding of Paul's attitude toward women in the Church; at most, it bears sad evidence to how quickly the Church retreated from Paul's more egalitarian practice. The case here is the same as regards 1 Corinthians 14:33b–36, which we also concluded was Deutro-Pauline.

CONCLUDING REFLECTIONS

Paul relied totally upon God for the strength to carry out his mission to the Gentiles. His unique theology of power in weakness graced him with the realization that only through the power of God at work in him could his human frailties and weaknesses be transformed and used to proclaim the gospel of Christ Jesus.

Paul understood that the success of his ministry came not in spite of his hardships and vulnerability but precisely because of them and through them. His suffering had opened the way for the power of his message and the Spirit (1 Corinthians 2; 2 Corinthians 4:7–18).[92] Paul was utterly convinced that in the midst of his weakness and suffering, the life of the risen Christ and God's extraordinary power were made visible in him (2 Corinthians 4:7–11, 16; 6:8–11).

Reflecting on his relationship to Christ, rather than listing his personal honors, Paul speaks of his disgraces, humiliations, and hardships, culminating in his confession of personal weakness (2 Corinthians 11:29).[93] Paul's personal weakness was primarily social; he endured the helplessness of one who had rejected status or power, and his humiliation was in the eyes of those who were honored with that same power and status.

In 2 Corinthians 12:9, distinguishing between his personal weakness and the power of Christ, Paul writes, "[The Lord] said to me, 'My grace is sufficient for you, for power is made perfect in weakness.'" In the paradoxical language of 2 Corinthians 12:10b, the distinction between Paul and Christ disappears, as Paul embraces Christ's reminder of the sufficiency of grace and declares, "For when I am weak, then I am strong."[94] In Paul's understanding of weakness and power, when a Christian is weak, her or his strength is the power of Christ active within.

Fundamentally, the emphasis for all members of the community of faith is on their relationship with Christ and their relationships with one another in Christ. Being in Christ calls each believer, woman and man, to utilize the gifts of the Spirit to promote understanding and love in the community of faith. Love is the greatest spiritual gift (1 Corinthians 13:13), and in Pauline communities "speaking the truth in love" (Ephesians 4:15 NRSV) is more highly

---

92. Mark Strom, *Reframing Paul: Conversations in Grace and Community* (Downers Grove, IL: InterVarsity, 2000), 111.

93. Ibid., 112.

94. Jan Lambrecht, *Second Corinthians*, Sacra Pagina 8 (Collegeville, MN: Liturgical Press, 1999), 208.

esteemed than authority and ritual.[95] Ultimately, the victory and the power of the cross are not through dominance, but through the awesome power of compassionate love, in and through solidarity with those who suffer.[96]

Paul's life and ministry were situated in the charismatic era of the early Church that preceded the development of any formal structure. This situation gave Paul an unimpeded freedom to embrace, utilize, and encourage the gifts and talents, as well as the leadership abilities, of both women and men.

Paul has been maligned by those who mistakenly believe that he held or encouraged views that diminished the leadership roles of women in the early Church. This chapter has demonstrated that Paul, in the undisputed letters, called, chided, and exhorted the Christian community to unity, a unity founded upon the baptism of every believer, both women and men. Paul believed that Christian unity resided in the grace of the Spirit, freely given to both women and men, and was essential for the life of the body of Christ, the Church.

The writings of Paul clearly indicate: (1) Women held governing positions in the early Christian communities. (2) Women exhibited great zeal and contributed greatly to the proclamation of the gospel. (3) Paul held women as his equals in the labor of announcing the gospel. (4) Paul is accustomed to submitting to women. (5) The work of the Church is not gender-specific. (6) No one, not even Paul himself, holds the designation of "most important" as apostle or missionary.[97]

Are there negative references to women in Paul? Some passages have been interpreted this way. However, scholarly research provides information about both the unique cultural contexts and customary practices that influenced the communities of faith to whom Paul wrote. Historically, some of the passages perceived as diminishing women have been cited partially or taken out of context. Such erroneous interpretations have yielded a caricature of Paul that has misled generations of both women and men who dismissed Paul and his writings based upon this misunderstanding. Contributing to the misunderstanding of Paul are several derogatory comments about

---

95. Strom, *Reframing Paul*, 137.

96. Johnson, "Redeeming the Name of Christ," 125.

97. Schottroff, *Let the Oppressed Go Free*, 36.

women that were handed down in Paul's name, but did not actually originate with Paul. Close examination of the texts demonstrates a marked contrast between the attitude of Paul himself and this later "Deutro-Pauline" tradition.

Paul's overwhelmingly positive treatment of women is substantiated by the numerous passages in which he asserts and acclaims the ministry of women and their leadership in the early Church. Paul cites roles for women as ministers that reveal a depth of respect and equality in ministry with men. Ultimately, an accurate reading of passages describing the many women co-workers who participated in the mission of the early Church reveals that Paul neither differentiated nor diminished women's leadership in ministry in relation to that of men.[98]

QUESTIONS FOR DISCUSSION

1. What images and words would you use to express your understanding of wisdom?

2. Who are some of the wisdom figures in your life and how have they influenced you?

3. Many women held positions of leadership in the first-century Church. What implications would this have had for the early Christian communities of faith? What implications does this have for Christian communities today?

4. Discuss how the entire community of faith is said to benefit from the gifts of the Holy Spirit.

5. What are some common misconceptions regarding Paul's writings about women? Clarify these misconceptions using material from this book.

---

98. MacDonald, "Reading Real Women Through the Undisputed Letters of Paul," 218.

chapter 5

Post New Testament to Modern Times

The previous chapters recalled the roles of women as ministers in the earliest Christian communities of the first century as recorded in the New Testament, and particularly in the writings of Paul. Historians, both secular and religious, also record the changing roles of women within the Christian Church from the first century to the present. These historical accounts, written almost entirely from a male perspective, illustrate both positive and negative perceptions regarding women in roles of ministry. As the early Christian communities of the first century grew, the organization and institutionalization of the Church gradually marginalized women's leadership. What follows is a brief overview of some of the significant female voices in the Church over the centuries, women who are role models because they embodied extraordinary faith in God, love of God, dedication to the people of God, and hope for the Church of God. These women courageously faced the challenges and obstacles set before them by the institutional Church and society at large.

THE FIRST FIVE CENTURIES

A wealth of material[1] describes the positions of ministerial leadership held by women during the first five centuries of Church history. This sacred treasure reveals the amazing stories of heroines whose names may be familiar but whose significance for the Church and the larger world is largely unrecognized.

---

1. Biblical research using a feminist hermeneutic, together with feminist recovery of Church history, provide scholarly reflection in the many resources made available within the last forty years. Numerous examples of these works are provided in the bibliography.

The positive contributions of women ministers in the Christian Church stand in tension with the historical practices of ecclesiastical patriarchy and misogyny. Within a relatively short period, approximately thirty years, the message of the resurrected Jesus to the women disciples to "go and tell" was dramatically changed. Male Christian leaders began to institute restrictions on women's participation in Christian discipleship.[2]

During the first century, women exercised roles beyond those described in the New Testament. For example, some women held positions of ministerial leadership within the house churches where Christians gathered for worship. Women and men were engaged in the missionary activities of proclaiming the gospel and caring for the poor, widows, orphans, and prisoners. Women held positions of authority and leadership in the Church. Titles such as *ruler of the synagogue, deacon, presbyter,* and *honorable woman bishop,* chiseled in tombstones from the early centuries, witness to this reality.[3] Inscriptions on monuments and buildings, as well as artistic sources, further corroborate the fact of women's leadership in the earliest Christian communities. One of the predominant figures in early Christian art found in Roman catacombs is the *orans,* a woman with her arms extended in prayer such as the mid-third century fresco of the *orans* painted in an alcove in the Priscilla Catacomb in Rome. The tomb epigrapha of Theodora, who lived in the fourth century, record that she was a protector of the law (*optima servatrix legis*) and a teacher of the faith (*fides magistra).*[4] These artifacts demonstrate the essential leadership roles that women held in the house churches. As authority figures who were widely accepted, these women engaged in teaching, in preaching, and in caring for the spiritual and temporal needs of the community.[5]

---

2. Sandra M. Schneiders, *The Revelatory Text: Interpreting the New Testament as Sacred Scripture* (Collegeville, MN: Liturgical Press, 1999), 182.

3. Laura Swan, *The Forgotten Desert Mothers: Sayings, Lives, and Stories of Early Christian Women* (Mahwah, NJ: Paulist Press, 2001), 6. See also Joan Morris, *The Lady Was a Bishop* (New York: The Macmillan Company, 1973).

4. Ute E. Eisen, *Women Officeholders in Early Christianity: Epigraphical and Literary Studies,* trans. Linda M. Maloney (Collegeville, MN: Liturgical Press, 2000), 94–95.

5. Karen Jo Torjesen, "The Early Christian *Orans*: An Artistic Representation of Women's Liturgical Prayer and Prophecy," in *Women Preachers and Prophets through Two Millennia of Christianity,* ed. Beverly Mayne Kienzle and Pamela J. Walker (Berkley, CA: University of California Press, 1998), 53.

As the early Church grew in size and power during the second and third centuries, it also took on a hierarchical structure that, ironically, began to reflect the Roman imperial structures of government and administration that periodically persecuted Christians. This growth, while positive in terms of increased followers, caused concern. Many disciples feared that the power connected to the institutionalization of the Church undermined the quest for holiness. Some disciples felt that the faith was being compromised and secularized as Christianity moved away from the house churches on the fringes of society to gather in larger public places and become part of mainstream Roman culture.[6]

The transition from early house church to later Roman hierarchy diminished women's authority. Fewer women ministers held positions of leadership, and participation of those women ministers was reduced significantly. Acculturation into the societal majority influenced the male leaders within the Christian Church to overlook Jesus' empowerment of women and to reject the leadership of women in public roles. This decrease in leadership roles for women in mainstream Christianity led to the movement of women to the desert and to the monastery, places that offered women opportunities to express a spiritual and physical autonomy similar to that available to women in the earlier house churches.[7]

The asceticism of the life in the desert and in the monastery was a means by which Christian women could gain freedom to live the spiritual life during the patristic era. The Fathers of the Church held that women who embraced celibacy were so radically different from other women that they functionally constituted a "third sex."[8]

During the final decades of the third century, a movement for greater asceticism and a simple life that afforded the opportunity to focus on prayer emerged in the Egyptian desert. Initially those who embraced this prayerful life did so as hermits. While this expression of spirituality continued, a more communal style of monastic life also evolved. The movement that included the "Desert

---

6. Swan, *The Forgotten Desert Mothers*, 9.

7. Ibid., 10.

8. Elizabeth A. Clark, *Women in the Early Church* (Collegeville, MN: Liturgical Press, 1983), 17.

Fathers" also included women known as "Desert Mothers." Monastic life was rooted in this movement and continued to develop through the ensuing centuries.

The call to monastic life, interwoven with a desire for asceticism, was based in the desire to leave behind distractions and to focus single-heartedly on the quest for God. This call was rooted as well in the desire to embrace Christ by living a countercultural, gospel-based way of life. The search for authenticity in their discipleship and a radical desire to embrace a life of holiness motivated laymen and laywomen to commit themselves to a monastic lifestyle.[9]

DEACONESSES

There is historical evidence that from the beginning of the early Christian communities of faith (from the first century through the fifth century) women commonly served in the role of deacon (deaconess). The Councils of Nicaea (325 CE) and Chalcedon (451 CE) addressed and clarified concerns about the ordination of deaconesses.[10] The nineteenth canon of the Council of Nicaea stated that deaconesses were to be counted as lay persons and they were to receive no ordination.[11] The fifteenth canon of the Council of Chalecdon determined that age 40 was to be the minimum age of deaconesses. This was to assure that deaconesses would not marry after they had received the "laying on of hands."[12]

The ministry of women deacons graced the early Christian Church. The Church consecrated these women and their ministry of service with an ordination ritual. A surviving written record describes one of the invocations prayed during the ordination of a deaconess. The bishop laid hands on the candidate and prayed,

> O eternal God, the Father of our Lord Jesus Christ, the Creator of man and of woman, who did fill with the Spirit

---

9. Thomas D. McGonigle and James F. Quigley, *A History of the Christian Tradition: From Its Jewish Origins to the Reformation* (New York: Paulist Press, 1988), 118.

10. Swan, *The Forgotten Desert Mothers*, 107.

11. Roger Gryson, *The Ministry of Women in the Early Church*, trans. Jean Laporte and Mary Louise Hall (Collegeville, MN: Liturgical Press, 1976), 48.

12. Ibid, 63.

Miriam, Deborah, Anna and Huldah,[13] who did not deem unworthy that your only-begotten Son should be born of a woman, who also in the tent of witness and in the Temple ordained women as keepers of your holy gates:[14] now look upon this your servant who is being ordained as a deaconess, and give her the Holy Spirit, and purify her from any defilement of the flesh and spirit,[15] so that she may worthily accomplish the work entrusted to her and to your glory and the praise of your Christ, with whom to you and to the Holy Spirit be glory and adoration forever. Amen![16]

The historical record of the growth of the Christian Church indicates that women were overseers (*episcopae*) of churches and Christian communities from the first century CE, a practice sustained throughout the first four centuries in diverse cultures. Only gradually, through the years, was women's leadership suppressed.[17] By the fourth century, the role of deaconess was no longer recognized in the Western Church either officially or liturgically, although in the Eastern Church the role was recognized until the eleventh century. Even so, some women continued in this ministry as evidenced by historical documents. For example, Helaria, daughter of Saint Remigius of Reims (d. 533), is mentioned in his will as the "deaconess."[18] Saint Olympias (d. 407), one of the closest friends and supporters of Saint John Chrysostom, was a wealthy and renowned deaconess in the fifth century.[19]

ABBESSES

As already noted, monastic settings offered women leadership opportunities not found in the secular world. Historical records demonstrate

---

13. Exodus 15:20–21; Judges 5; Luke 2:36–38; 2 Kings 22:14–20.

14. Exodus 38:8 and 1 Samuel 2:22.

15. 2 Corinthians 7:1.

16. *Didascalia et Constitutiones Apostolorum*, 8.20, cited in Clark, *Women in the Early Church*, 181.

17. Morris, *The Lady Was a Bishop*, 3.

18. Swan, *The Forgotten Desert Mothers*, 108.

19. Jeannine E. Olsen, *One Ministry Many Roles: Deacons and Deaconesses Through the Centuries* (St. Louis, MO: Concordia Publishing House, 1992), 22.

egalitarian practices in the monasticism of the seventh century with regard to women's authority. "Thus at the close of the seventh century there existed in the province of Kent alone five religious settlements governed by abbesses who added this title to their signatures, or who, judging from the place given to them, ranked in dignity below the bishops but above the presbyters (*presbyteri*), whose names follow theirs in the list. From the wording of the charter we see that men who accepted the tonsure and women who received the veil were at this time classed together."[20] Note that *presbyteri* are, in fact, priests (our word "priest" derives from this term); apparently these abbesses held a higher rank than that of the priests. One notable example of a powerful abbess is Hilda of Whitby (Britain), who called and hosted in her monastery the Synod of Whitby in 664 that determined the pattern for setting the celebration of Easter in Britain.

As the monastic tradition continued to develop in the High Middle Ages, 1100–1300, the abbots and priors were given some of the same responsibilities and powers possessed by bishops; so, too, were abbesses and prioresses. Within the limits of her own abbey, the abbess had the power of a bishop and bore a crozier as a sign of her rank.[21]

The practice of abbesses bearing a crozier continues even today. The titles of *Episcopa*, *Sacerdota Maxima*, *Praeposita*, and *Custos* of churches conferred on women indicate that they had some of the powers of a bishop in relationship to the churches and people within their jurisdiction.[22]

Intricately interwoven into the fabric of the historical record of abbesses through the centuries is their alignment with political power that often was both fragile and tenuous. In some cases, the alliance of abbesses with political rulers provided their office both political and religious power. One example of the extent of the power and influence of abbesses is shown in circumstances where they took the place of the feudal lord.

---

20. Lina Eckenstein, *Woman Under Monasticism: Chapters on Saint-Lore and Convent Life Between A.D. 500 and A.D. 1500* (1899; reprint New York: Russell and Russell, Inc., 1963), 87.

21. Ibid., 203.

22. Morris, *The Lady Was a Bishop*, 138.

The cultural and political influence of the abbesses extended into the fifteenth century, particularly in the locales where their abbeys were established. Significantly, in contexts where there were communities for men and for women, the abbess was often the superior of both. Such was the case of the order of St. Bridget founded in Sweden in the 1300s.

Additionally, abbesses were given great power over the members of their respective communities, and in some circumstances the local bishop would confer with them. The members of the convent were completely under the authority of the abbess, whose decisions and rulings were absolute. The rule of the religious order sometimes referred to the abbess as a sovereign.[23]

MYSTICS

Throughout the centuries women mystics have been, and continue to be, significant in the life of the Church. They have been highly esteemed for their profound life of prayer, their visions of the Divine, their healing powers, their ministries, and their spiritual advice. While they were excluded from ecclesial offices within the institution of the medieval Church, women mystics functioned as authority figures.[24] They influenced the lives of individual men and women who sought out their spiritual insights and advice. On more than one occasion, they affected entire countries, and even the universal Church, as they counseled men of prominence including emperors, kings, and popes.

Four of the women mystics who enhanced the life of the Church in their day, and who continue to inspire the spiritual life of the Church today, are Hildegard of Bingen, Catherine of Siena, Julian of Norwich, and Teresa of Avila.

Hildegard of Bingen

Hildegard of Bingen (1098–1179), a German abbess, made significant contributions to the spiritual life of the Church. Her varied talents were reflected in her numerous accomplishments as physician, composer and musician, artist, scientist, mystic, visionary, theologian,

---

23. Ibid., 388.

24. Barbara J. MacHaffie, *Her Story: Women in Christian Tradition* (Philadelphia, PA: Fortress Press, 1986), 59–60.

and writer. She authored a book entitled *Scivias*, which describes her mystic visions and contains her astounding and vibrant symbolic illustrations.[25] Her copious correspondence with popes, kings, and emperors provides us with insights about the tumultuous political and religious events of her historical era.

The abbey founded by Saint Hildegard is at the top of a hill overlooking the lush and verdant vineyards that cover the hillsides of Bingen, Germany, with a panoramic and majestic view of the Rhine and its powerful, swift current. The sacred power of the divine feminine, a theme in Hildegard's writings, exudes from the life-giving presence of the rich fertile earth and the creative power of water in the fundamental elements of nature in this region. Perhaps it is this simple and natural presence of God that inspired Hildegard to celebrate the sacred feminine[26] and to embrace its power.

The abbey church with its simple décor and engaging feminine representations of the sacred can still be seen. On the walls between the archways of the side aisle of the nave in the abbey church are painted larger-than-life portraits (four to five meters tall) of some of the women who served as abbess in the nearly nine-hundred-year history of the abbey, established in 1147. Several of the abbesses in these paintings are depicted in full religious habit, wearing a miter, and holding a crozier.[27] The crozier—and miter, where present—derive from the fact that the authority of the abbess over the community under her jurisdiction is the same as the authority of a bishop.

Catherine of Siena

Catherine of Siena (1347–1380) was a laywoman accepted into the Dominican Third Order at the age of sixteen. Although she spent

---

25. Robert Ellsberg, *All Saints: Daily Reflections of Saints, Prophets and Witnesses for Our Time* (New York, NY: The Crossroad Publishing Company, 1997), 406.

26. Both in her writings and in her paintings, Hildegard portrays her high regard for the beauty of the feminine. On occasion, she encouraged her sisters to dress in tiaras and flowing white robes, a fact documented in correspondence that criticized her for this practice.

27. According to a sister contacted at the Abtei St. Hildegard, or Abbey of St. Hildegard, in Eibingen, Germany, there are actually ten women who lived during the first millennia of the Church's history who are pictured holding a crozier, and two of the ten are also wearing a miter. Their names are: Adelgundis, Bilhildis, Edeltrudis, Erentudis, Herlindia, Irmengardis, Lioba, Odilia, Thecla, and Walburga.

much of her time enclosed in her room in prayer, she began to focus her attention on the wider world and the universal Church after an experience in 1374 in which she heard a call from God. Despite the restrictions on women of her time, Catherine felt compelled to embrace the ministries of caring for the sick, preaching, and reconciliation. She believed that she received her commission from God and therefore did not rely on an official commission from the Church.[28]

Eventually Catherine came to be revered as a public figure. Unable to write, she dictated numerous letters that were sent to men in leadership positions, including monarchs and Popes Gregory XI and Urban VI. In these letters, she spoke directly, fervently, and courageously, counseling these prominent men on the importance of moral integrity in their actions and in the performance of their duties.

From 1309 to 1377, the papal court was in Avignon rather than in Rome during a period known as the Avignon papacy, sometimes called the "Babylonian Captivity of the Church." Here the pope, as well as members of the papal court, fell under the authority of Philip IV, king of France. During this time, the papacy lost its credibility in political and cultural affairs, and most importantly, its moral authority.[29] Catherine was gravely troubled with this disintegration in Christian leadership.

Catherine journeyed to Avignon to meet personally with Pope Gregory XI. She boldly challenged him and was unrelenting in her insistence that he return the papacy to its rightful place in Rome. Gregory recognized the truth of what she spoke, as well as the obvious holiness that animated her.[30] Moved by her appeal, he returned to Rome, dying shortly thereafter. Pope Urban VI, who succeeded Gregory, remained in Rome, but his pontificate was scarred by conflicts in the Italian city-states, particularly in the city of Florence.[31] A second pope was elected in Avignon and thus the Church was burdened with two rival, and eventually warring, pontiffs. Although

---

28. Mary Catherine Hilkert, *Speaking With Authority: Catherine of Siena and the Voices of Women Today* (Mahwah, NJ: Paulist Press, 2001), 31.

29. Joanne Turpin, *Women in Church History: 20 Stories for 20 Centuries* (Cincinnati, OH: St. Anthony Messenger Press, 1990), 111.

30. Ibid., 113.

31. Ellsberg, *All Saints*, 189.

the situation of the Church was calamitous, Catherine remained unwavering in her loyalty to Pope Urban VI, believing that, in spite of his shortcomings, he was in fact the duly consecrated pontiff.[32]

In the year 1378, within a three-month period, Catherine dictated her spiritual classic, *Divine Dialogue*, to Raymond of Capua, a priest who was her spiritual advisor and friend.[33] In this book, Catherine offers spiritual guidance and reflects on her fervent prayer life. In 1970, this courageous and holy woman mystic of the fourteenth century was the second of only three women[34] in the history of the Roman Catholic Church to be declared a Doctor of the Church.

Julian of Norwich

Very little is known about Julian of Norwich (1342–1416), who lived as an enclosed anchoress in her later life. A woman mystic from England, she dedicated her life to prayer and penance as a hermit.[35] Julian writes of her spiritual visions expressing the depth of God's goodness and compassion in her book *Showings*, also known as *Revelations of Divine Love*. Julian uses feminine imagery and writes of the motherhood of God.[36] The gift of her spirituality is her profound insight that the God who created human beings out of love and who redeemed humanity by suffering love desires to be united with that same humanity.[37]

Teresa of Avila

Teresa of Avila (1515–1582), known for her mystical writings, was the foundress of seventeen convents. She helped to inspire her confessor and colleague, John of the Cross, to form a male branch of the Discalced (shoeless) Carmelites. Teresa was also a religious reformer, an author, a spiritual director, a master of Christian prayer, and a mystic.

---

32. Turpin, *Women in Church History*, 113.

33. Bernard McGinn, *The Doctors of the Church: Thirty-Three Men and Women Who Shaped Christianity* (New York, NY: The Crossroad Publishing Co., 1999), 131.

34. The other two women who have been named Doctors of the Church are Teresa of Avila in 1970 and Therese of Lisieux in 1997.

35. McGonigle and Quigley, *A History of the Christian Tradition*, 173.

36. Ibid., 174.

37. Ellsberg, *All Saints*, 212.

Though the voice of women was ignored and discredited in sixteenth-century Spain, the light of Christ was vibrant within her and thus her prayer and her words were respected.[38] One of Teresa's correspondents during the time she was refounding the Carmelite Order was King Philip II of Spain. He intervened on her behalf when some of her opponents reported her writings to the Spanish Inquisition.[39]

Teresa's deep spirituality and intimate relationship with God are expressed in the delightful sense of humor evident in her prayer. On one occasion, Teresa was riding in a donkey cart when it overturned and threw her into a muddy river. She complained to God and heard a voice within say, "Don't complain about the muddy water, Teresa; this is how I treat my friends." Teresa replied to God: "Yes, Lord, and that is why you have so few of them!"[40]

In 1577, Teresa authored *The Interior Castle*, the result of her mature reflection on the spiritual life and the culmination of her teaching on prayer. Teresa authored this work as an act of obedience in response to the order of Father Jerome Gratian (1545–1614), her spiritual director, confessor, and religious superior.[41]

Of the many and varied legacies that Teresa bestowed upon the Church, one of the most profound was her insight that women have a unique way of expressing and sharing their spirituality and their relationship with God with one another. "Teresa assumes that 'the language used between women' will be readily understood by her sisters. This last comment is important because, in Teresa's day, ordinarily, the individual sister spoke primarily with the male priest/confessor about the progress of her spiritual life. To his credit, Gratian seems to have understood that sometimes the gender difference, with its consequent difference in life experiences, contributed to a gap in understanding a matter as intimate as a sister's prayer life."[42]

38. Ibid., 449.

39. Joanne Turpin, *Women in Church History: 21 Stories for 21 Centuries* (Cincinnati, OH: St. Anthony Messenger Press, 2007), 157.

40. Ibid., 450.

41. Roseanne McDougall, "From *The Cloud* (Unknown Author) to *The Castle* of Teresa of Avila: Teresian Metaphor as Transition from 'Unknowing' to 'Being Known,'" in *Women Christian Mystics Speak to Our Times*, ed. David B. Perrin (Franklin, WI: Sheed & Ward, 2001), 134.

42. Ibid., 135.

Teresa of Avila was the first woman in the history of the Roman Catholic Church to be distinguished as a Doctor of the Church.[43]

THE LATER CENTURIES

The Reformation period was a tumultuous and complex era in the life of the Church. While some perceive this age as a time of revolt and disloyalty, others observe that the Reformers were striving to rectify abuses in the Church and to challenge the Church to reclaim its moral integrity by living the vision of Jesus and the Christian values recorded in the writings of the New Testament.

One of the most notable women of this era was Katharina von Bora Luther (1499–1525), whose husband was the renowned Martin Luther (1486–1546). Katharina was sent to the convent at age three by her father following her mother's death. Hearing and coming to believe the biblical teaching of Martin Luther, Katharina, along with eleven other nuns, escaped the convent. Two years later she married Luther and together they had six children and also raised four orphans. The Luther family became a model for Christian family life. In addition to the household management, Martin encouraged and guided Katharina in her study of the Scripture. Katharina died six years after her husband and was buried in Torgau, Germany.

During the period of the Reformation, prominent women leaders emerged in the Anabaptist movement. This reform movement, begun in 1525, was relatively egalitarian in its beginnings. The movement focused on the presence and activity of the Holy Spirit within each individual believer, both male and female, as well as one's personal responsibility to yield to the working of the Holy Spirit in one's life. While there is no evidence that these prominent women held official leadership roles within the congregations, some are known to have actively engaged in proselytizing and sharing their religious beliefs. Indeed, some of these women were imprisoned and even martyred for their beliefs.[44] It is precisely because the majority of these women were in the background that they were able to provide the leadership

---

43. Ellsberg, *All Saints*, 450.

44. C. Arnold Snyder and Linda A. Huebert Hecht, eds., *Profiles of Anabaptist Women: Sixteenth-Century Reforming Pioneers*, Studies in Women and Religion 3 (Waterloo, ON: Wilfrid Laurier University Press, 1996), 409.

to sustain and continue this "underground movement."[45] Some of the better-known women from this movement were: Helena von Freyberg of Münichau, Austria († 1545),[46] Ursula Jost of Strasbourg, Austria (c. 1500),[47] Barbara Rebstock of Strasbourg, Austria (c. 1500),[48] and Hille Feicken of Münster, Germany († 1534).[49]

To respond to the crisis caused by the Reformation, Pope Paul III convened the Council of Trent (1545–1563). The council met in three different sessions during these eighteen years. Among the council's accomplishments were the official declaration that there are seven sacraments instituted by Christ, the re-emphasis of the position that God's grace can overcome the effects of original sin, and the institution of the seminary system for the formation of the clergy.[50]

The Renaissance and the Reformation dramatically affected the prevailing attitudes regarding women in all aspects of life: political, economic, cultural, social, and religious. During the sixteenth century, Aristotle's philosophy competed with the teachings of Jesus as men in power embraced a low opinion of women and denied them positions of leadership. Monks began to reassert the position initiated in the eleventh-century Gregorian Reforms that they could not be under obedience to a layperson (i.e., someone who was not ordained). The ideal of servant leadership, where the greatest is called to serve the least, declined. The resulting practices removed women from secular professions and trades and drove them out of the service of the Church.[51]

Notable events in the eighteenth century, including the Great Awakening/Enlightenment, the American Revolution, and the French Revolution, as well as those in the nineteenth century, particularly the Jacksonian Period, the Market Revolution that culminates in the Industrial Revolution, and the resulting plagues that occurred in the burgeoning populations in the newly urbanized areas, created a

45. Ibid., 8.

46. Ibid., 124–40.

47. Ibid., 273–78.

48. Ibid., 278–84.

49. Ibid., 288–97.

50. McGonigle and Quigley, *A History of the Christian Tradition*, 203.

51. Morris, *The Lady Was a Bishop*, 101.

climate that generated and expanded the opportunities for the cultivation of women's ministry and spirituality. The rise of women's involvement in society outside the home was most evident and acceptable in Church work and its resultant social activism—namely, women's involvement in both the temperance and abolition movements. The Protestant denominations most often represented in these movements were Quakers, Unitarians, and Methodists.

During these two centuries, numerous religious communities for women emerged and flourished. Many of these religious communities were founded by widows, others by single women who desired to embrace more fully a simple life of service to God expressed in prayer and in service for others, particularly the poor. Some of the foundresses during this time included Maria Anna Brunner (1764–1836), foundress of the Sisters of the Precious Blood; Elizabeth Ann Seton (1774–1821), foundress of the Sisters of Charity; Catherine McAuley (1778–1841), foundress of the Sisters of Mercy; and Julie Billiart (1751–1816), foundress of the Sisters of Notre Dame de Namur.

Most of these women, who stepped outside of the religious, cultural, political, and societal norms of their *milieu*, are revered as heroines to this day. They were mystics, healers, artists, wisdom figures, spiritual advisors, teachers, and, most importantly, women of intense prayer who embraced the hunger and thirst for deeper faith, informed by knowledge and wisdom. Their passion for God led them to live courageous lives divergent from and sometimes contrary to the culture of their historical times and the norms established for women by the Church.

In addition to those whose stories are well known, there are countless generations of wives and mothers, vowed women religious and single laywomen, and other wise women who followed Christ, embraced the call of discipleship, and ministered to their families as well as to the Christian communities of faith.

QUESTIONS FOR DISCUSSION

1. Discuss some of the leadership roles that women held in the early Church in the period after the apostles. What is learned from their experience?

2. What does it mean to lead a monastic life? Can men and women adopt this lifestyle today? How?

3. Discuss the leadership roles that women held in the Church in the Middle Ages. Does their experience have value for us? Explain.

4. Discuss some of the pivotal female figures of the twelfth through the sixteenth centuries. Why, and in what ways, were they significant?

5. Why is it important to understand history and to learn about its impact on religion?

6. What is the significance of religious artwork depicting women of faith as either feminine or androgynous?

7. How have the changing norms of society influenced the roles of women in the Church?

8. What characteristics of these historic women role models are significant today? What makes them significant?

epilogue

The venue for discussion about the Apostle Paul and his writings concerning the role of women in ministry has moved for me from the kitchen table of my childhood home to classroom tables in colleges and universities. I have integrated and deepened the wisdom of my first teachers with my own study and reflection on the sacred texts as well as the writings of Scripture scholars.

Feeling the presence of my ancestors and their passion for discussing the Bible, from time to time I share with my students what I fondly refer to as "wisdom from the great hillbilly theologian, my dad." The words of Paul ring true as the discussion continues: "For I received from the Lord what I also handed on to you . . . " (1 Corinthians 11:23). Finally, I humbly echo Paul as I share a final blessing: "I am confident of this, that the one who began a good work in you will continue to complete it until the day of Christ Jesus" (Philippians 1:6).

glossary

anchoress: a woman who withdraws from secular society to a life of seclusion for religious reasons. The anchoresses lived one of the earliest forms of monastic life and were considered hermits.

Before the Common Era (BCE): the period before the birth of Jesus Christ. It replaces the designation "before Christ" (BC).

celibate: one who chooses to remain unmarried and who abstains from sexual intercourse, often for religious reasons.

charism: a distinctive gift or grace given by God to an individual, meant to be used for the good of others.

Common Era (CE): the time beginning with the birth of Jesus Christ. It replaces the designation "the year of the Lord," *anno Domini* (AD) in Latin.

doctor of the Church: in Latin the word *doctor* means "teacher." In the Catholic Church, the title is given posthumously by a pope to those who made what are considered important contributions to theology or the understanding of doctrine. Thirty-three persons have been granted this distinction; three of them are women.

eschaton: the end of time, the end of the world. Also, *eschatological*.

exegesis: the process of critically examining and analyzing the meaning of literary texts, performed by *exegetes*. Also *exegetical*.

feministic hermeneutic: a way of viewing, interpreting, and explaining biblical texts with a particular focus on women and women's issues.

hermeneutic: a method or principle of interpretation and explanation of a text.

kenotic: self-emptying, especially referring to the sacrifice of Jesus referred to in Philippians 2:7.

koinonia: the fellowship among members of a Christian community that expresses itself in acts of charity and service to others.

methodology: the practices and procedures carried out by those engaged in the study of a particular discipline.

misogyny: hatred or contempt for females.

orans: a female figure praying with outstretched arms, commonly found in early Christian art, including on the walls of the catacombs in Rome.

Parousia: the second coming of Christ in glory.

paterfamilias: Latin for "father of a family," it refers to the father or head of a tribe or household.

patriarchy: a social system in which the father is the head of the family and genealogy is traced only through the father.

patristic era: the first eight centuries (CE) of Christianity, when the fathers of the Church shaped its creeds, doctrines, and traditions.

patristics: the study of the lives and writings of the fathers of the Church.

pericope: a complete passage, unit, or story within the Bible.

sapiential: related to wisdom.

bibliography

Achtemeier, Paul J., Joel B. Green, and Marianne Meye Thompson. *Introducing the New Testament: Its Literature and Theology.* Grand Rapids: Eerdmans, 2001.

Anderson, Sherry Ruth, and Patricia Hopkins. *The Feminine Face of God.* New York: Bantam Books, 1991.

Angelou, Maya. "Still I Rise." In *Maya Angelou: Poems*, 154. New York: Bantam Books, 1996.

Bauckham, Richard. *Gospel Women: Studies of the Named Women in the Gospels.* Grand Rapids: Eerdmans, 2002.

Bellis, Alice Ogden. *Helpmates, Harlots and Heroes.* Louisville: John Knox, 1992.

Bergant, Dianne. "Biblical Foundations for Christian Ministry." In *Together in God's Service: Toward a Theology of Ecclesial Lay Ministry*, National Conference of Catholic Bishops, Subcommittee on Lay Ministry, Committee on the Laity, 87–102. Washington, DC: United States Catholic Conference, 1998.

Berquist, Jon L. *Reclaiming Her Story.* St. Louis: Chalice, 1992.

Bevans, Stephen B. *Models of Contextual Theology.* Maryknoll, NY: Orbis, 2000.

Boff, Leonardo. *The Maternal Face of God.* San Francisco: Harper & Row, 1987.

Breault, William. *The Lady from Dublin.* Boston, MA: Quinlan Press, 1986.

Bristow, John Temple. *What Paul Really Said about Women: An Apostle's Liberating Views on Equality in Marriage, Leadership, and Love.* San Francisco: Harper & Row, 1988.

Brown, Raymond E. *The Churches the Apostles Left Behind.* Mahwah, NJ: Paulist Press, 1984.

Brown, Raymond E. Brown, Joseph A. Fitzmyer, and Roland E. Murphy, eds. *The New Jerome Biblical Commentary.* Englewood Cliffs, NJ: Prentice Hall, 1990.

Bunson, Matthew, Margaret Bunson, and Stephen Bunson. *Our Sunday Visitor's Encyclopedia of Saints, Updated.* Huntington, IN: Our Sunday Visitor, Inc., 1998.

Byrne, Brendan. *Romans.* Sacra Pagina 6. Collegeville, MN: Liturgical Press, 1996.

Canon Law Society of America. *Code of Canon Law: Latin-English Edition.* Washington, DC: Canon Law Society of America, 1983.

Chittister, Joan, D. *Scarred by Struggle, Transformed by Hope.* Grand Rapids: Eerdmans, 2003.

Clark, Elizabeth A. *Women in the Early Church.* Message of the Fathers of the Church, ed. Thomas Halton, vol. 13. Collegeville, MN: Liturgical Press, 1983.

Collins, Raymond F. *These Things Have Been Written: Studies on the Fourth Gospel.* Louvain, Belgium: Peeters Press, and Grand Rapids: Eerdmans, 1990.

———. *First Corinthians.* Sacra Pagina 7. Collegeville, MN: Liturgical Press, 1999.

Cozzens, Donald. *Sacred Silence: Denial and the Crisis in the Church.* Collegeville, MN: Liturgical Press, 2002.

Crenshaw, James L. *Old Testament Wisdom: An Introduction.* Atlanta: John Knox, 1981.

Diamant, Anita. *The Red Tent.* New York: Picador, 1997.

Diaz, Zoila. "Baptism and the Baptized in Church Leadership." In *Together in God's Service: Toward a Theology of Ecclesial Lay Ministry,* National Conference of Catholic Bishops, Subcommittee on Lay Ministry, Committee on the Laity, 51–69. Washington, DC: United States Catholic Conference, 1998.

Donahue, John R., and Daniel J. Harrington. *The Gospel of Mark.* Sacra Pagina 2. Collegeville, MN: Liturgical Press, 2002.

Dunn, James D. G. *The Theology of Paul the Apostle.* Grand Rapids: Eerdmans, 1998.

Eckenstein, Lina. *Woman under Monasticism: Chapters on Saint-Lore and Convent Life between A.D. 500 and A.D. 1500.* New York: Russell and Russell, 1963.

Eisen, Ute E. *Women Officeholders in Early Christianity: Epigraphical and Literary Studies.* Translated by Linda M. Maloney. Collegeville, MN: Liturgical Press, 2000.

Elliott, Terri. "Making Strange What Had Appeared Familiar." *The Monist* 77, no. 4 (1994): 424–33.

Ellsberg, Robert. *All Saints: Daily Reflections of Saints, Prophets and Witnesses for Our Time.* New York: Crossroad, 1997.

Fee, Gordon D. *God's Empowering Presence: The Holy Spirit in the Letters of Paul.* Peabody, MA: Hendrickson, 1994.

———. *Paul, the Spirit, and the People of God.* Peabody, MA: Hendrickson, 1996.

Flannery, Austin, ed. *Vatican Council II: The Basic Sixteen Documents.* Revised translation in inclusive language. Northport, NY: Costello, 1996.

Fox, Zeni. "Ecclesial Lay Ministers: An Overview." In *Together in God's Service: Toward a Theology of Ecclesial Lay Ministry,* National Conference of Catholic Bishops, Subcommittee on Lay Ministry, Committee on the Laity, 3–22. Washington, DC: United States Catholic Conference, 1998.

Furnish, Victor Paul. *The Moral Teaching of Paul: Selected Issues.* Nashville: Abingdon, 1985.

Getty-Sullivan, Mary Ann. *Women in the New Testament.* Collegeville, MN: Liturgical Press, 2001.

Gillman, Florence M. *Women Who Knew Paul.* Collegeville, MN: Liturgical Press, 1992.

Gregory the Great. *Homilia 33.* In *XL Homiliarum in Evangelia.* PL 76:1238–46.

Grey, Mary. *Feminism, Redemption and the Christian Tradition.* Mystic, CT: Twenty-Third Publications, 1990.

Gryson, Roger. *The Ministry of Women in the Early Church.* Translated by Jean Laporte and Mary Louise Hall. Collegeville, MN: Liturgical Press, 1976.

Harrington, Daniel J. *The Gospel of Matthew.* Sacra Pagina, Vol. 1. Collegeville, MN: Liturgical Press, 1991.

Hilkert, Mary Catherine. *Speaking With Authority: Catherine of Siena and the Voices of Women Today.* Mahwah, NJ: Paulist Press, 2001.

Hock, Ronald F. *The Social Context of Paul's Ministry: Tentmaking and Apostleship.* Minneapolis, MN: Augsburg Fortress Press, 2007.

Hoffman, James R. "Ecclesial Lay Ministry in a Local Church." In *Together in God's Service: Toward a Theology of Ecclesial Lay Ministry*, National Conference of Catholic Bishops, Subcommittee on Lay Ministry, Committee on the Laity, 158–67. Washington, DC: United States Catholic Conference, 1998.

Huels, John M., "Special Questions on the Diaconate." *Liturgical Ministry* 13 (Winter 2004): 1–9.

Jansen, Katherine Ludwig. *The Making of the Magdalene: Preaching and Popular Devotion in the Later Middle Ages.* Princeton, NJ: Princeton University Press, 2000.

John Paul II, Pope. *On The Dignity and Vocation of Women (Mulieris Dignitatem).* Washington, DC: United States Catholic Conference, 1988.

———. *Letter of Pope John Paul II to Women.* Boston: Pauline Books and Media, 1995.

Johnson, Elizabeth A. *She Who Is.* New York: Crossroad, 1992.

———. "Redeeming the Name of Christ." In *Freeing Theology: The Essentials of Theology in Feminist Perspective*, ed. Catherine Mowry LaCugna, 115–37. New York: HarperCollins, 1993.

Johnson, Luke T. *The Writings of the New Testament.* Philadelphia: Fortress, 1986.

———. *The Gospel of Luke.* Sacra Pagina 3. Collegeville, MN: Liturgical Press, 1991.

———. *The Acts of the Apostles.* Sacra Pagina 5. Collegeville, MN: Liturgical Press, 1992.

Karris, Robert J., ed. *The Collegeville Bible Commentary.* Collegeville, MN: Liturgical Press, 1992.

Keener, Craig S. *Paul, Women and Wives: Marriage and Women's Ministry in the Letters of Paul.* Peabody, MA: Hendrickson, 2001.

Kirk, Martha Ann. *Women of Bible Lands: A Pilgrimage to Compassion and Wisdom.* Collegeville, MN: Liturgical Press, 2004.

Kittel, Phyllis M., *Staying in the Fire: A Sisterhood Responds to Vatican II.* Bolder, CO: Woven Word Press, 2009.

Koperski, Veronica. "Feminist Concerns and the Authorial Readers in Philippians." *Lovain Studies* 17 (1992): 269–92.

———. *What Are They Saying About Paul and the Law?* Mahwah, NJ: Paulist Press, 2001.

Kraemer, Ross Shepherd, and Mary Rose D'Angelo, eds. *Women and Christian Origins.* New York: Oxford University Press, 1999.

Kroeger, Catherine Clark, and Mary J. Evans, eds. *The IVP Women's Bible*. Downers Grove, IL: InterVarsity, 2002.

Lambrecht, Jan. *Second Corinthians*. Sacra Pagina 8. Collegeville, MN: Liturgical Press, 1998.

Lampe, Peter. *From Paul to Valentinus: Christians at Rome in the First Two Centuries*. Translated by Michael Steinhauser. Minneapolis, MN: Augsburg Fortress Press, 2003.

MacHaffie, Barbara J. *Her Story: Women in Christian Tradition*. Philadelphia: Fortress, 1986.

Maddocks, Fiona. *Hildegard of Bingen: The Woman of Her Age*. New York: Doubleday, 2001.

Marchal, Joseph A. *The Politics of Heaven: Women, Gender, and Empire in the Study of Paul*. Minneapolis, MN: Augsburg Fortress Press, 2008.

Markey, John J. *Creating Communion: The Theology of the Constitutions of the Church*. Hyde Park, NY: New City, 2003.

Matera, Frank. *Galatians*. Sacra Pagina 9. Collegeville, MN: Liturgical Press, 1992.

Mays, James L., ed. *The HarperCollins Bible Commentary*. New York: HarperCollins, 2000.

McDougall, Rosanne. "From *The Cloud* (Unknown Author) to *The Castle* of Teresa of Avila: Teresian Metaphor as Transition from 'Unknowing' to 'Being Known.'" In *Women Christian Mystics Speak to Our Times*, ed. David B. Perrin, 129–42. Franklin, WI: Sheed & Ward, 2001.

McFague, Sallie. *Models of God*. Philadelphia: Fortress, 1987.

McGinn, Bernard. *The Doctors of the Church: Thirty-Three Men and Women Who Shaped Christianity*. New York: Crossroad, 1999.

McGonigle, Thomas D., and James F. Quigley. *A History of the Christian Tradition: From Its Jewish Origins to the Reformation*. New York: Paulist Press, 1988.

Meeks, Wayne A. *The First Urban Christians: The Social World of the Apostle Paul*. New Haven: Yale University Press, 1983.

Meyers, Carol, Toni Craven, and Ross S. Kramer, eds. *Women in Scripture: A Dictionary of Named and Unnamed Women in the Hebrew Bible, the Apocryphal/Deuterocanonical Books and the New Testament*. Grand Rapids: Eerdmans, 2001.

Moloney, Francis J. *The Gospel of John*. Sacra Pagina 4. Collegeville, MN: Liturgical Press, 1998.

Morris, Joan. *The Lady Was a Bishop*. New York: Macmillan, 1973.

Murnion, Philip J. *New Parish Ministers: Laity and Religious on Parish Staffs*. New York: National Pastoral Life Center, 1992.

Murphy, Roland E. *The Tree of Life: An Exploration of Biblical Wisdom Literature*. Grand Rapids: Eerdmans, 2002.

Murphy-O'Connor, Jerome. *Paul: A Critical Life*. New York: Oxford University Press, 1996.

Nouwen, Henri. *The Wounded Healer*. Garden City, NY: Doubleday, 1972.

Perkins, Pheme. *Reading the New Testament*. Mahwah, NJ: Paulist Press, 1988.

Pettegree, Andrew, ed. *The Reformation World*. New York: Routledge, 2000.

Portefaix, Lilian. *Sisters Rejoice: Paul's Letter to the Philippians and Luke-Acts as Seen by First-Century Philippian Women*. Coniectanea Biblia, New Testament Series 20. Stockholm, Sweden: Almqvist & Wiksel International, 1988.

Reid, Barbara E. *Choosing the Better Part?* Collegeville, MN: Liturgical Press, 1996.

Reilly, Patricia Lynn. *A God Who Looks Like Me*. New York: Ballantine Books, 1995.

Richard, Earl J. *First and Second Thessalonians*. Sacra Pagina 11. Collegeville, MN: Liturgical Press, 1995.

Roetzel, Calvin J. *Paul: The Man and the Myth*. Personalities of the New Testament. Minneapolis, MN: Augsburg Fortress Press, 1999.

Ross, Susan A. "God's Embodiment and Women." In *Freeing Theology: The Essentials of Theology in Feminist Perspective*, ed. Catherine Mowry LaCugna, 185–209. New York: HarperCollins, 1993.

Ruether, Rosemary Radford. *Sexism and God-Talk: Toward a Feminist Theology*. Boston: Beacon, 1993.

———. *Women and Redemption*. Minneapolis, MN: Fortress, 1998.

Schmidt, Kimberly D., Diane Zimmerman Umble, and Steven D. Reschly, eds. *Strangers at Home: Amish and Mennonite Women in History*. Baltimore, MD: The Johns Hopkins University Press, 2002.

Schneiders, Sandra M. *The Revelatory Text: Interpreting the New Testament as Sacred Scripture*. Collegeville, MN: Liturgical Press, 1999.

———. *Written That You May Believe: Encountering Jesus in the Fourth Gospel.* New York: Crossroad, 2003.

Schottroff, Luise. *Let the Oppressed Go Free: Feminist Perspectives on the New Testament.* Translated by Annemarie S. Kidder. Louisville: Westminster John Knox, 1993.

———. *Lydia's Impatient Sisters: A Feminist Social History of Early Christianity.* Translated by Barbara and Martin Rumscheidt. Louisville: Westminster John Knox, 1995.

Schreiter, Robert J. *Constructing Local Theologies.* Maryknoll, NY: Orbis, 1999.

Schüssler Fiorenza, Elisabeth. *In Memory of Her: A Feminist Theological Reconstruction of Christian Origins.* New York: Crossroad, 1989.

———. *But She Said: Feminist Practices of Biblical Interpretation.* Boston: Beacon, 1992.

———. *Discipleship of Equals: A Critical Feminist Ekklesia-logy of Liberation.* New York: Crossroad, 1993.

———. *Wisdom Ways: Introducing Feminist Biblical Interpretation.* Maryknoll, NY: Orbis, 2001.

Snyder, C. Arnold, and Linda A. Huebert Hecht. *Profiles of Anabaptist Women: Sixteenth-Century Reforming Pioneers.* Studies in Women and Religion 3. Waterloo, Ontario, Canada: Wilfrid Laurier University Press, 1996.

Steinfels, Peter. *A People Adrift: The Crisis of the Roman Catholic Church in America.* New York: Simon & Schuster, 2003.

Stone, Merlin. *When God Was a Woman.* New York: Barnes and Noble, 1976.

Strom, Mark. *Reframing Paul: Conversations in Grace and Community.* Downers Grove, IL: InterVarsity, 2000.

Swan, Laura. *The Forgotten Desert Mothers: Sayings, Lives, and Stories of Early Christian Women.* Mahwah, NJ: Paulist Press, 2001.

Torjesen, Karen Jo. *When Women Were Priests: Women's Leadership in the Early Church and the Scandal of Their Subordination in the Rise of Christianity.* San Francisco: HarperCollins, 1995.

———. "The Early Christian *Orans*: An Artistic Representation of Women's Liturgical Prayer and Prophecy." In *Women Preachers and Prophets through Two Millennia of Christianity,* ed. Beverly Mayne Kienzle and Pamela J. Walker, 42–56. Berkley: University of California Press, 1998.

Trible, Phyllis. *God and the Rhetoric of Sexuality*. Philadelphia: Fortress, 1978.

———. *Texts of Terror*. Philadelphia: Fortress, 1984.

Turpin, Joanne. *Women in Church History: 20 Stories for 20 Centuries*. Cincinnati: St. Anthony Messenger Press, 1990.

United States Catholic Conference of Bishops. "Together in God's Service: Toward a Theology of Ecclesial Lay Ministry." Papers from a Colloquium, 1998.

———. "Lay Ecclesial Ministry: The State of the Questions." Report of the National Conference of Catholic Bishops Subcommittee on Lay Ministry, 1999.

Vinje, Patricia Mary. *Praying with Catherine of Siena*. Winona, MN: Saint Mary's Press, 1990.

Whitehead, James D. and Evelyn Eaton Whitehead. *Method in Ministry: Theological Reflection and Christian Ministry*. Franklin, WI: Sheed & Ward, 1999.

Winter, Bruce W. *After Paul Left Corinth: The Influence of Secular Ethics and Social Change*. Grand Rapids: Eerdmans, 2001.

Wright, Nicholas T. *What Saint Paul Really Said: Was Paul of Tarsus the Real Founder of Christianity?* Oxford: Lion, 1997.

———. *Paul: In Fresh Perspective*. Minneapolis, MN: Augsburg Fortress Press, 2005.

Zagano, Phyllis. *Holy Saturday: An Argument for the Restoration of the Female Diaconate in the Catholic Church*. New York: Crossroad, 2000.

Zetterholm, Magnus. *Approaches to Paul: A Student's Guide to Recent Scholarship*. Minneapolis, MN: Augsburg Fortress Press, 2009.

index